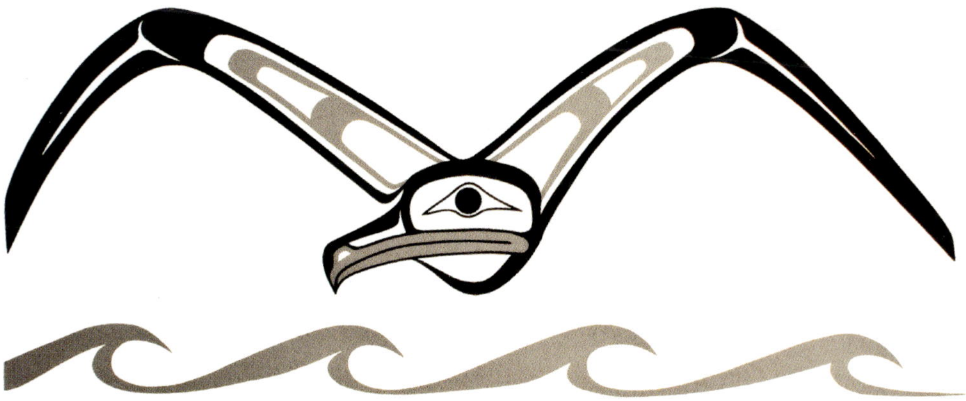

THE BEST OF

ROY HENRY VICKERS

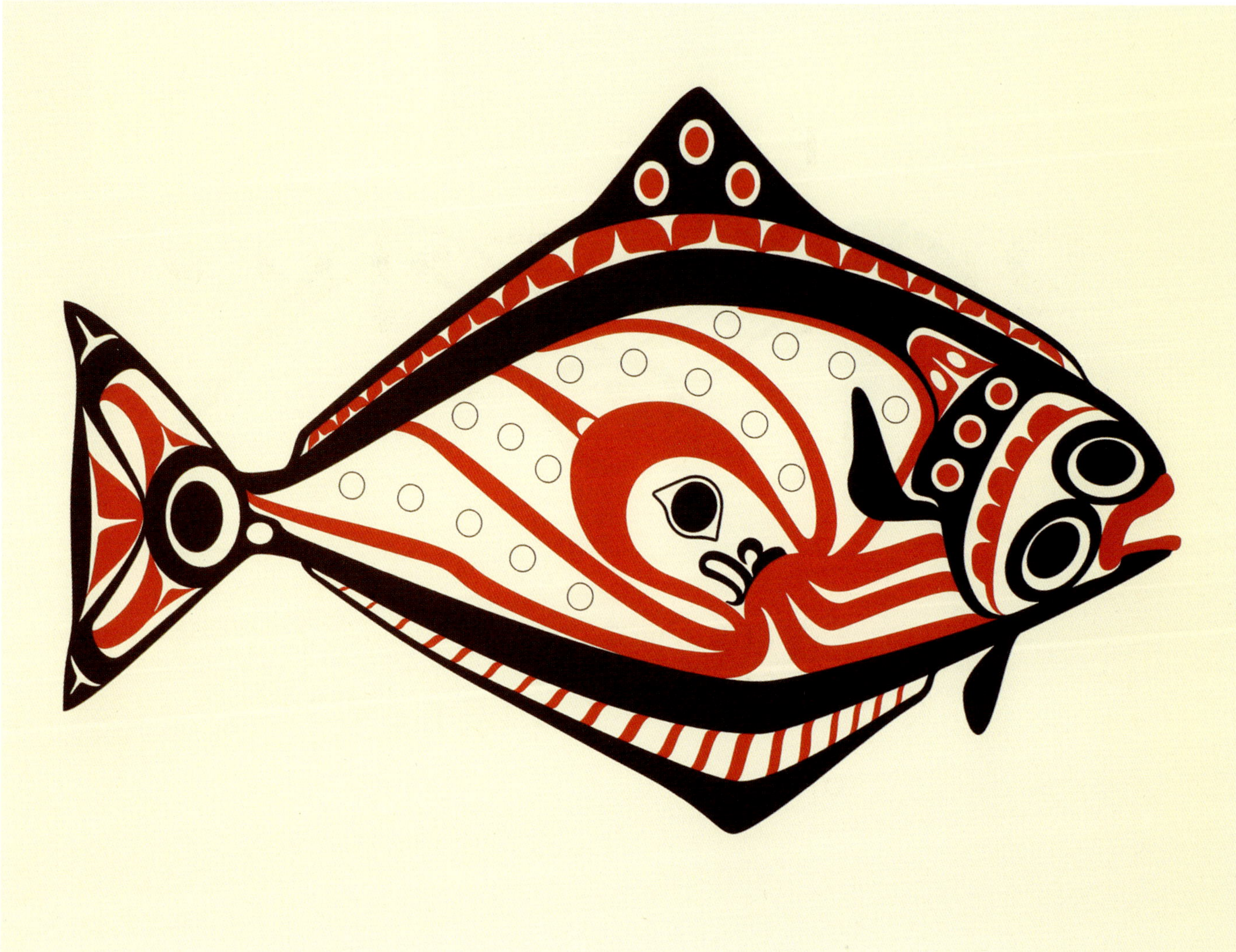

Halibut 2007

THE BEST OF

ROY HENRY VICKERS

80 SELECTED WORKS

FOREWORD BY LUCKY BUDD

HARBOUR
PUBLISHING

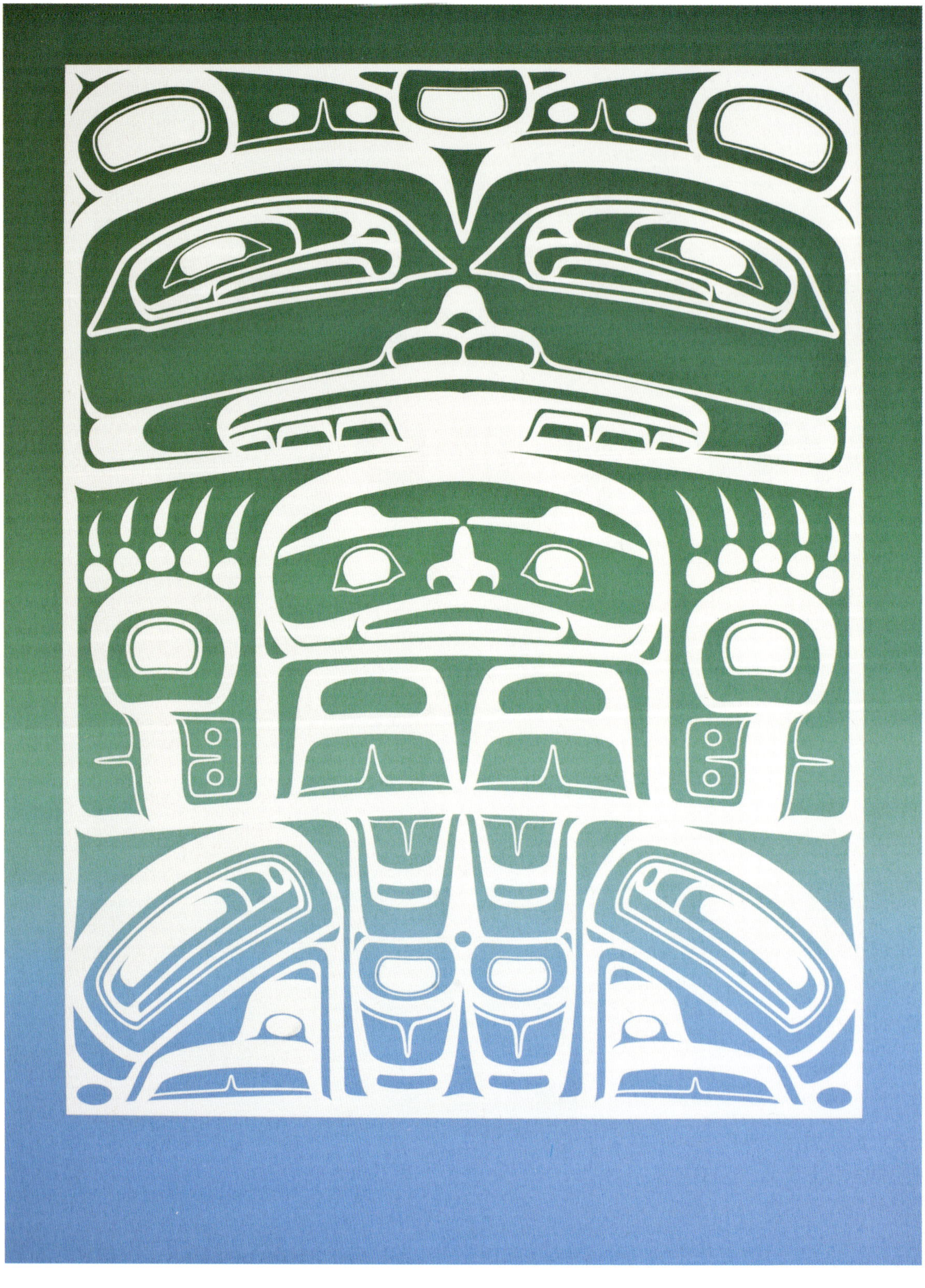

Contents

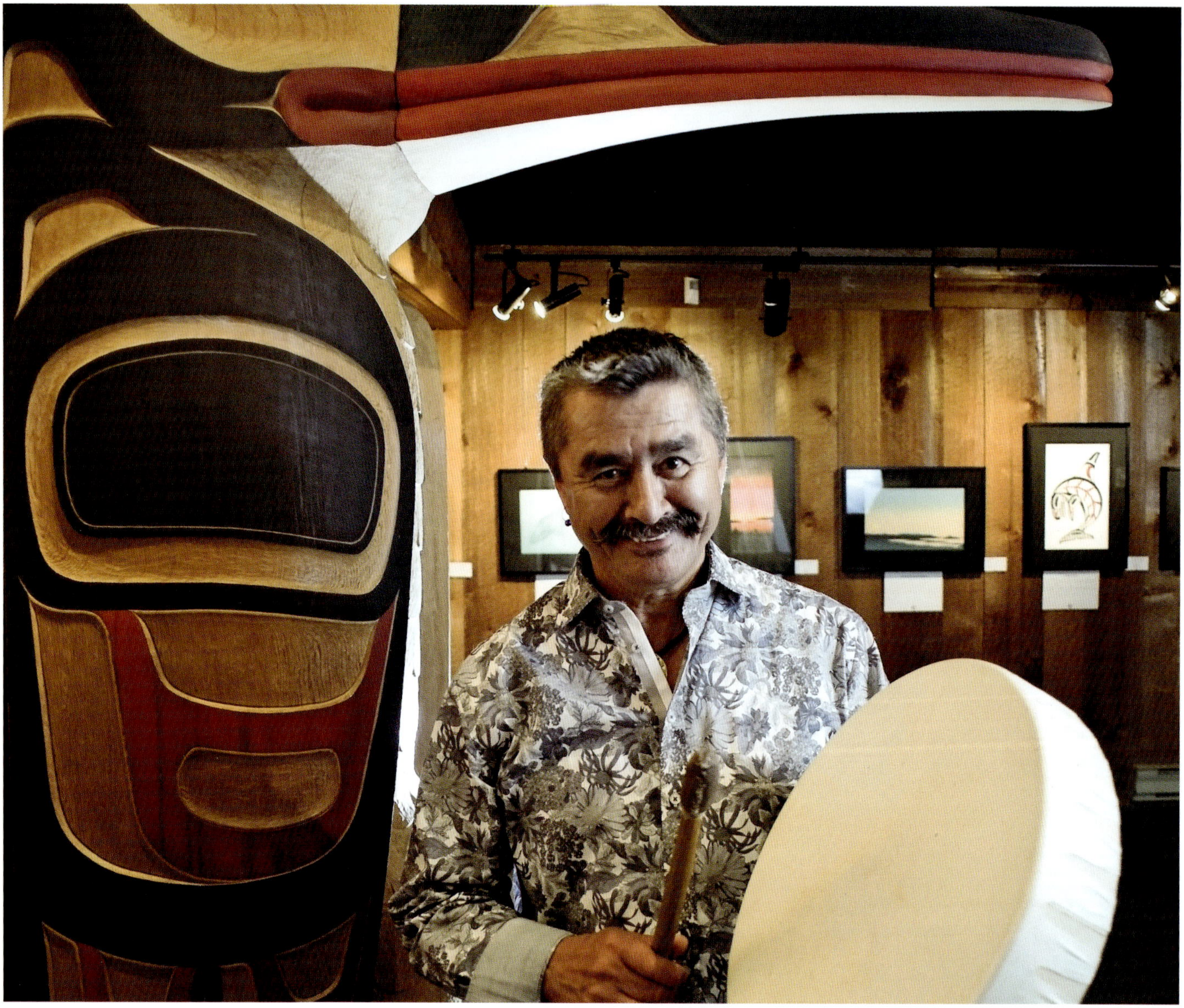

Foreword

LUCKY BUDD, 2026

JUNE 4, 2026, marks Roy Henry Vickers' eightieth birthday—this milestone also celebrates fifty-two years that Roy has been a professional artist. The coming together of these two anniversaries seemed like a perfect time for a celebration of Roy's life, his artwork and his unsurpassed contribution to educating the world about the nations and land of the Northwest Coast.

Roy is a gifted visionary who only works from inspiration. Let me tell you, when inspiration hits, it is like a spark of joy. Roy has explained many times how the word *inspiration* comes from the Latin word *inspiratus*. He taught me to look again, and *re-spect* the relationship of the English words *inspiration* and *respiration*. *Inspiratus* contains the Latin for words *breathe* and *spirit*, and it means the breath of the Creator coming into you, or respirating you. No wonder it is such a joyous experience; it is divine!

Over our years of friendship and collaboration, Roy and I have had countless conversations about music, songwriting and storytelling. I have also had the privilege of watching Roy draw many times from a place of inspiration. There is a musicality, ease and rhythm in his work similar to watching the world's best guitar players practise their craft. There is a magic that you can feel when you witness a master create. It almost appears to be effortless. It is as if they are a conduit: the art comes through them, and all they have to do is get out of the way, trust in what they know and let it be.

Roy is among the world's great storytellers. In fact, all of the images in this book—and all of the works Roy has ever created—tell a story. I am so lucky that he is always willing to share a story. The learning is immense. Each of his works contain layer upon layer of meaning and teachings for those who are open to hearing the stories. They come from a place of the Four Directions and the four-faces of the teacher, the healer, the visionary and the leader.

In his fifty-two years as a professional artist, Roy has created nearly four hundred separate limited edition prints. In celebration of his birthday, it is a true joy to share a selection from this body of work: eighty images for eighty years. Many happy returns, my friend!

Roy holds a drum at Eagle Aerie Gallery in Tofino. *Chris Pouget*

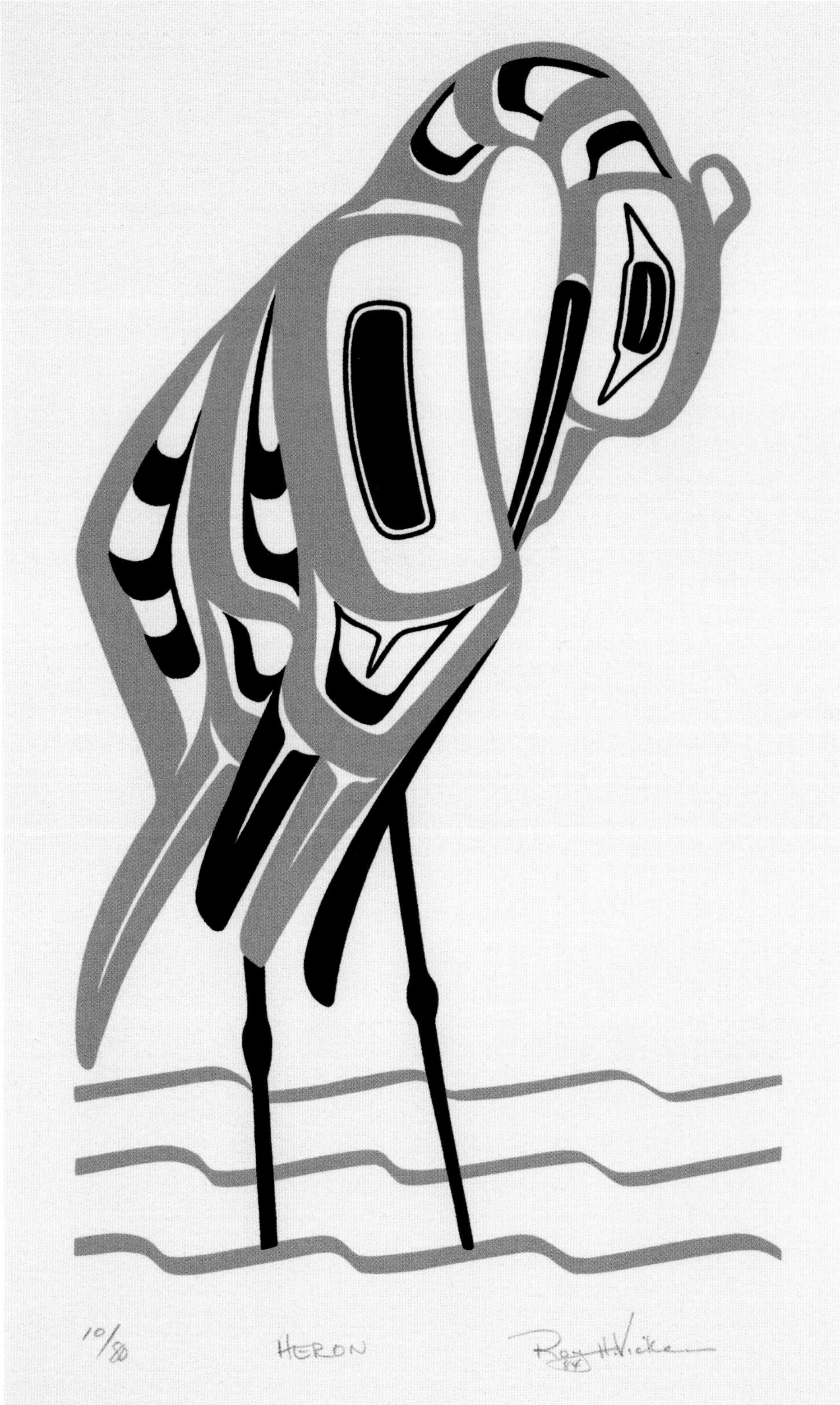
10/80
HERON

Introduction

ROY HENRY VICKERS, 2026

I WAS BORN IN 1946 on the banks of the Nass River in northern British Columbia in a village known today as Laxgalts'ap; in the old days it was called Greenville. My mother wanted to go to the hospital in Prince Rupert; however, the tide was out and the boats were all dried up on the beach. An old lady who was in charge of the midwives paid a visit to my mom and said to her, "Ayn, ayn—no, no. He's going to be born here." Mom had them clean up the backroom in the schoolhouse, and that's where I was born. I've been in school ever since.

My mother's parents immigrated to this country from England. Her mother came from Scarborough and her father came from Birmingham. They met and married in Eastern Canada and started working their way across the country. Mom was born in Moose Jaw, Saskatchewan. After her birth, the family moved to Vancouver, BC, where Mom grew up.

My father's mother, Kathleen Collinson, was from a long line of women that go back many generations in the ancient village of Kitkatla. My father's father, Henry Vickers, was from Waglisla, also known as Bella Bella, BC. My father's grandfather was from Haida Gwaii, and so my Northwest Coast Indigenous roots are Heiltsuk, Haida and Kitkatla—Kitkatla today is recognized as a nation unto itself.

After my birth, my parents moved back to Kitkatla, and that's where I grew up in this ancient village, which is over five thousand years old. My old teacher and friend Wilson Duff believed Kitkatla is the oldest continuously inhabited site in all of North America.

When I was born, there was no bassinet or crib; they wrapped me up and put me in this little cardboard box filled with blankets. My dad looked down at the box and started to laugh. My mom asked, "What is it, Art?" and Dad said, "Look at the box." Mom looked down and on the end of the box was printed "Heinz 57." It's so true, my lineage includes many nations both Northwest Coast and European. I love Heinz 57 ketchup to this day.

As a child, I grew up with music all around me. We had no electricity, no radios, but there were guitars, harmonicas, saxophones, violins and a marching band. I grew up with music and many storytellers who would invite me to visit and tell me stories. I love telling stories.

One of my earliest childhood memories was from when I was four years old. I took a trip by boat from our home in Kitkatla to Prince Rupert before making the long journey south to Vancouver to visit my mother's parents at their home on Cree St.

Grandpa was a good storyteller. He would share stories from his own life. He used to tell me stories about lying about his age so that he could go fight in the Boer War in South Africa in the last days of the 1890s. He was only 17 when he left England. He told me that while he was aboard a ship on his way to war, it was his job to look after the horses.

I also remember him reading *Legends of Vancouver*, a book by E. Pauline Johnson. He had a sense that my brother and I were half-breed children growing up in this world, and that we should know about our ancestry on our father's side. I remembered when I was much older that he cared enough to read stories about the Sechelt people written by E. Pauline Johnson with the permission of Chief Joe Capilano.

In Kitkatla, our food supply was the ocean. I learned winds and tides, moons and seasons for gathering food. It was a beautiful childhood.

I loved to draw. I got in trouble at school, and I used to have to write on the blackboard "I will not draw in math class" a hundred times. That teacher took away my drawings so I would pay attention and do my best in school. Many years later, a woman came into my art gallery and introduced herself as Dr. Marlene Hunter, and she said, "You won't remember me as Dr. Hunter, but you'll remember me as Miss Buckle." Miss Buckle said, "I took your drawings away and put them in a box. I've tried to find those drawings many times over the years, but I can't find them." I said, "Well, Miss Buckle, if you ever find those drawings, I will trade you for anything you want in this art gallery." She went away and I never saw her again.

When I was nine years old, my mom and dad decided we would move from Kitkatla to Hazelton. Mom got a job teaching in the school and Dad worked in the logging industry. I didn't like this new place; however, there were horses. My first ride on a horse was probably the second day in Hazelton. I have been in love with horses ever since. Horses were part of our lives; they roamed loose over the land. When we wanted to ride all we needed was a rope. We would catch our favourite horse and ride. No saddles, no bridles, just ride.

When I was twelve, a horseman named Al Benson approached my parents and asked if he could teach me how to ride his racing horses. I became a jockey and I spent hundreds and hundreds of hours riding horses. They became this great love of my life and taught me many things.

I stayed with horses until I was sixteen, when I went away to Three Hills, Alberta, to attend a high school there. I had a hard time being away from home. I missed my family, and when I finally caught up to them, they had moved to Victoria.

I was with my family, but I wasn't home. Hazelton was my home. Kitkatla was my home. I missed the north country and returned every year. The move to Victoria was difficult; I was lost in this big city school called Oak Bay High School. I came across discrimination for the first time in my life in Victoria and I didn't know what it was; discrimination was not part of my life. I was different from everyone else and I wanted to know what that difference was. Who did they see?

My art teacher, Mr. West, knew that I was dealing with discrimination and I did not like studying European art; he apologized that he had to teach me the curriculum. There were no books on Northwest Coast Indian art. Mr. West directed me to the museum where I could study the art of my father's people. Every weekend, I went down to the museum to watch Henry Hunt carve. Henry introduced

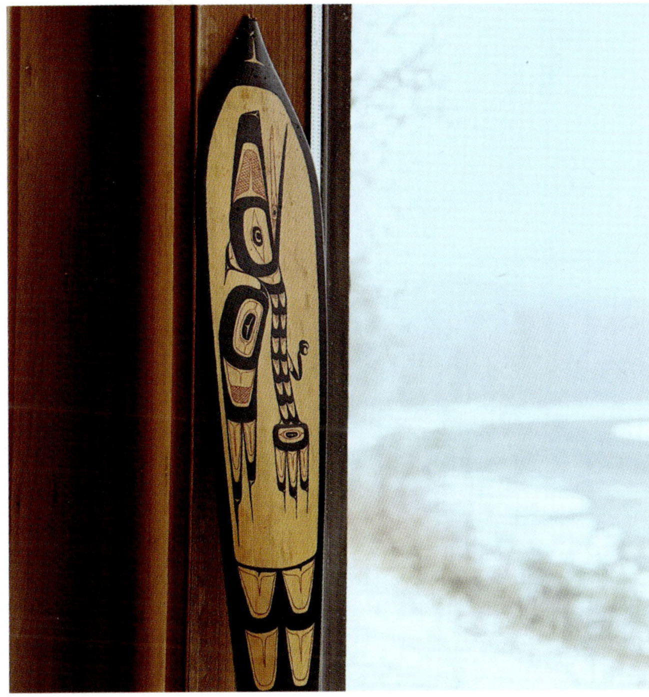

me to Wilson Duff, the head of the BC Provincial Museum, which became my new school. I took it upon myself to learn the art of my father's ancestors.

I graduated from Oak Bay High School and I applied to the RCMP because they were mounted police and they travelled all over the world. I dreamed of being one of the riders and I would get paid to ride horses all over the world. When I failed my medical and learned I could not join the RCMP, I went back to Mr. West and told him that I was partially colourblind. He said, "No wonder you use the strong colours that you use. That's what you see, and that's good. That's your difference—that's your uniqueness." I applied to the Saanich Fire Department and I got a job there and I continued to study my art. My friends at the

Roy designed and carved this paddle in 1972 for his application into the Gitanmaax School of Northwest Coast Indian Art at 'Ksan.

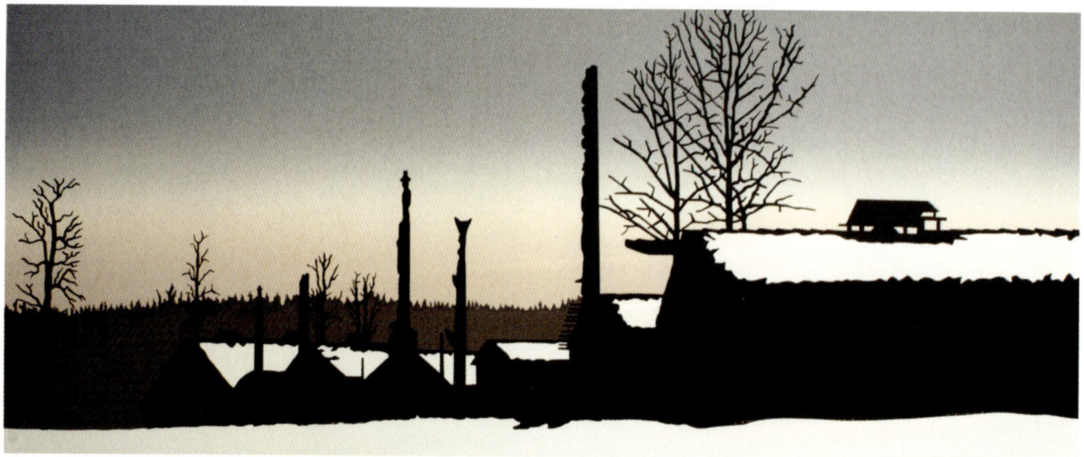

fire department told me that I was wasting my time there and I should be an artist. I got to draw there in the quiet times; I argued with them that I had a good job and I could be an artist anyway. They told me if I kept working and making money that I would not work as hard at my art. At that time, Henry Hunt told me that I should go away to Hazelton and study at the Gitanmaax School of Northwest Coast Indian Art at 'Ksan.

I applied to the school and was accepted. So, I took a leave of absence from the fire department and returned to the community of Hazelton that I loved. I loved studying there, so I spent hours working. I carried my sketchbook everywhere I went. There is a part of me that woke up; it was just waiting to come into reality. After dinner I went back to the school to draw. On the weekends, I asked permission to go and study and work there on Saturdays, even though it was closed. I would go home to sleep and then I was there again the next morning. It was in Hazelton where I learned to draw ovoids (the core shape in Northwest Coast art), and learned the language of the ovoid, the u-shape, the s-shape, and the primary, secondary and tertiary colours. These are the foundation of the art of the Northwest Coast. It all came to me so fast. It was like somebody just turned a page in the book of my life and there it all was.

In 1973, after the first school year ended, I went back to the fire department. While I was there, I was doing my artwork whenever I could at slack time. I continued to get pressure from my friends at work that I should just be an artist.

Before I went back to school in 1974, I travelled to Mexico for a holiday. One day in Mexico, I was sitting on the beach playing my guitar and harmonica. Four Mexican men came up to me and started speaking to me in Spanish. I said, “Momento, momento, no hablo español.” They looked at me thinking that I was Mexican. Then they heard me speaking Spanish and they wondered what

Hazelton (2004) shows where Roy attended art school at 'Ksan.

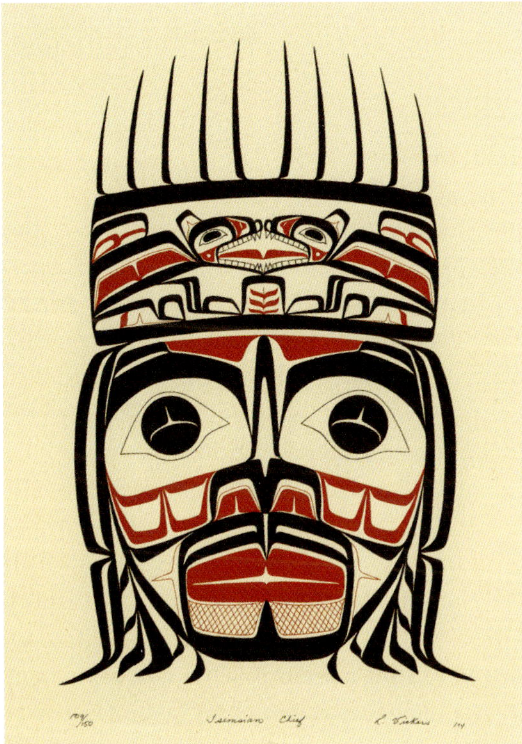

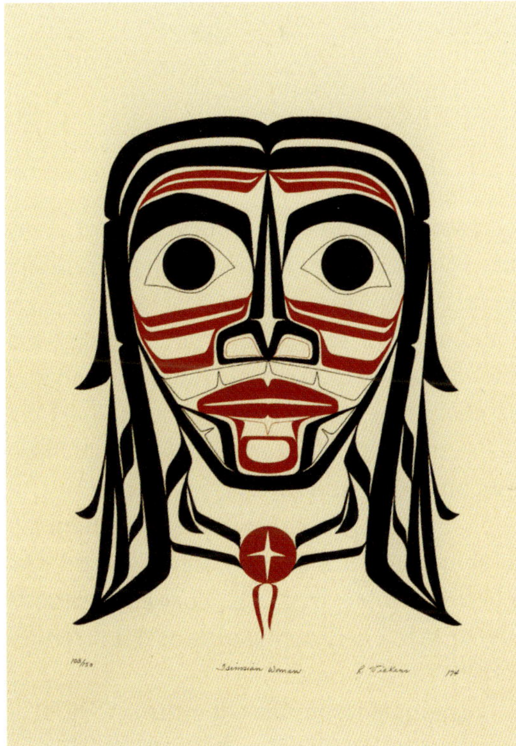

was going on. I realized this, so I said quickly, "I come from Canada and I learned to speak Spanish in school." Then they looked at me with their mouths open, wondering *Who is this guy*? I said, "I'm a Canadian Indian. My mother was white and my father was Indian. So, actually, I'm Mexican in a way because media y media, half and half, that's what Mexican means, half Spanish and half Indian." We became friends. They were actually a four-piece band and they invited me to come and practise music with them. I ended up joining them and playing my guitar and harmonica in the band. I enjoyed my time with these four guys. Over the next six weeks I travelled to their village, I rode horses on their ranch and then I had to look at travelling home.

While I was heading back in the desert between Nogales and Arizona, I pulled over to the side of the road, walked out into the desert and fell to my knees. I wondered why I was so afraid of becoming an artist and leaving a good job. I started to cry. I realized that I had just been in a country where there was no unemployment insurance, there was no welfare, yet the people were happy. I was no longer afraid, and I made up my mind to call the fire department and tell them I wasn't coming back. I knew I was going to be an artist for the rest of my life.

Tsimshian Chief (left) and *Tsimshian Woman* were Roy's first prints after graduation, released in the summer of 1974.

I was determined to work very hard at my art. Two prominent artists in the community were Walter Harris from Kispiox and Earl Muldon from Hazelton. They became my friends and helped me outside of the school by showing me how they worked as artists. There was another man, Victor Mowat, who was an artist, and he had made a beautiful bentwood box. He came to me and asked me to paint it for him because he believed I was a better painter than him. That request gave me so much self-confidence and a stronger resolve to work hard.

I graduated from the Gitanmaax School of Northwest Coast Indian Art in June of 1974 and returned to Victoria. I created two limited edition prints, *Tsimshian Chief* and *Tsimshian Woman*. I took the ideas directly from my sketchbook at 'Ksan. Those two prints, in editions of 150 each, sold out in two weeks. I knew I was going to be an artist for the rest of my life.

My artistic world went into overdrive at this time; I travelled to Victoria and Vancouver monthly to visit galleries and tell stories of my creations. I was asked to teach Northwest Coast Indian art in night school classes at the University of British Columbia and loved to share the knowledge. Dr. Ames, head of the Museum of Anthropology, asked if I would put together an exhibition at the museum. I was the first of many artists to have a one-person exhibition of Indigenous art at the UBC Museum of Anthropology in Vancouver.

In 1977, I was invited to Ottawa during the Silver Jubilee celebrations of Queen Elizabeth II. I was invited as one of three hundred young Canadians who had achieved excellence in the arts and sciences. I met many talented Canadians and Her Majesty as well.

During this time I worked with a number of Indigenous artists and created a copper for the National Museum of Ethnology in Osaka. I also sold a complete collection of fine art prints to that museum. This was very exciting for me because two of my favourite artists in the world are Hokusai and Hiroshige, both from Japan.

In the beginning, every gallery owner or manager wanted to hear the stories for each creation. When my work became popular, nobody wanted to hear the stories and I began to feel like a commodity instead of a storyteller/teacher. I decided to withdraw from the world of selling art. I returned to the ocean and Kitkatla as a gillnet fisherman. One of my friends, Ron Hamilton, suggested I look at the world through the lens of a camera and I carried my Pentax Spotmatic II everywhere I went. Sunsets on the sea were my favourite subjects. I loved being back where I grew up; I heard more stories from the old people. I love the ocean.

In 1980 I fished all over the coast of BC and ended the season in Tofino. I met an old friend, Henry Nolla, and he talked me into staying for the winter to teach him to carve totems. He was a Spanish/Swedish man who was a gifted artist and sculptor. I fell in love with Tofino living beside the ocean. I returned to a world of creativity, paintings, limited edition fine art prints and sculptures. In 1982 I created the canoe series (p. 25–28). The series consisted of two two northern canoes and two southern canoes—because I was living in the south, I paid my homage to the Nuu-chah-nulth people. At this time in my career, I was struggling with moving away from traditional Indian art, and wanted to do something contemporary because I'm a contemporary person.

Elegy (p. 25) was the first one, and it was about winter. With *Elegy* I did snow for the first time, I did trees for the first time, and I did foreground, mid-ground, and background for the first time. It was *Elegy* that set me solidly on this new artistic journey that I was on.

Chief's Dream (p. 26) was the next piece in the series and it represented spring. With *Chief's Dream*, I thought, *I'm going to do a northern canoe going back to Kitkatla, and the eagle and the whale and the raven and the wolf are going to be paddling the canoe with the chief sitting in the bow.* I thought of my hero Hiroshige, and the way he was able to draw rain. This piece was actually going to be called *Supernatural Visitors*. People weren't ready for supernatural visitors at the time, so I changed the name to *Chief's Dream*.

I was challenged with the summer piece. I was afraid that my colour-blindness would prevent me from doing a sunset, so I jumped ahead to work on my piece for the fall, *The Westcoasters* (p. 27). Spring and fall rain were easy for me, as was winter snow, but I had no idea how to do a summer piece. I knew I had to capture a sunset, but I thought, *how am I going to do it? I'm colour-blind and I know it now. I've never done a sunset in my life.* I went to my collection of slides and put all my favourite sunset shots together in one carousel. One by one, I went through them, over and over again. Finally, something started to gel in my mind. I saw the grey lines of *Westcoast Sunset* (p. 28) separating red, orange, yellow, light blue and darker blue, and there it was with the silhouette of a Kitkatla canoe. It was magic. The image shows a canoe coming back home and saluting the sun setting.

The business people in Tofino began to pressure me to open a gallery. I was challenged to be a gallery owner and businessman and reluctantly opened Eagle Aerie Gallery above the Schooner Restaurant in Tofino. On rainy days all the hoteliers sent people to the gallery. I was inspired to build a bigger gallery and one of my friends told me his parents would sell me a corner lot on the main street. My brother Art owned Vickers Construction. Art and I designed the gallery and we built it. So it is that on April Fool's Day in 1986 I opened Eagle Aerie Gallery in Tofino.

In those days I had postcards of my art printed at Fleming Printing in Victoria. I had an exhibition of my art at Emily Carr's gallery. My art teacher Mr. West came to my exhibition at the Emily Carr House; we stood together looking at *Digging Clams* (p. 33) and he gave me a little nudge and asked me, "Do you recall what I said to you in art class about individual styles?" I replied, "Yes, you said that if I worked really hard to find out who I was and where I came from, and I created from that place, I would create what nobody else in this world could because each person is unique; we are all individuals. You said, 'Maybe one day you will hear someone say, I saw your sunset, or I saw your clouds or your water.'" He said, "Good for you. Well, you have to tell me what inspired you to put that canoe in the very front of *Digging Clams*. It was a stroke of genius." I laughed and said, "Well, it wasn't a stroke of genius. My memory is that I was this little boy and my job was to stand by the boat because we dig clams at a low tide, and while the people are digging clams, the tide's coming in, and my responsibility was to make sure that the boat didn't drift away. So, I stood by the boat, watching the people digging clams." He just said, "Well, that's my favourite piece."

In October 1986 I was honoured with a show in the Art Gallery of Greater Victoria. There were two other exhibitions there at the same time, Emily Carr and Hokusai, two of my favourite artists. During this time I was encouraged to put all my stories together with images and write a book, so it is that *Solstice: The Art of Roy Henry Vickers* was published in 1988. I had to self-publish as I could not find a publisher who would take it. I believe there were four editions of *Solstice* published and sold out, and I loved writing stories. Victoria was the subject of a series of prints in 1987; they were my tribute to the city that provided so much knowledge and support for my growth as an artist. (*Trial Island*, on p. 44, is from the Victoria series.)

The city of Vancouver also played a major role in my career as an artist. It was there that I studied at the Museum of Anthropology, where I had a large exhibition of my art. It was there that most of the galleries were that I sold my art to. I worked with the large printing companies to produce my books. One day I was working on a book, and this young fellow came in with my book *Solstice* in his hand.

Solstice 1996 (1996) shows the facade Roy designed and the Salmon Totem that Roy carved at Saanich Commonwealth Place on Vancouver Island, BC.

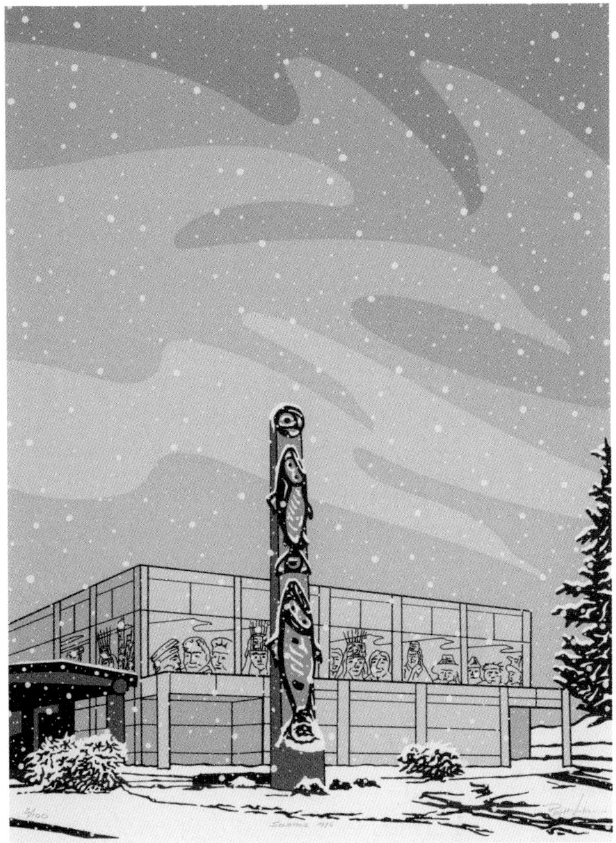

He introduced himself as Frank O'Neill's assistant at the Vancouver International Airport. Frank O'Neill wanted to know if I could help bring the feeling of my book into the Vancouver International Airport. My answer was yes and I was invited to YVR to meet Frank O'Neill.

I began another life as artistic adviser on the board of YVR. A plane would come to Tofino and pick me up and fly me to the airport. I would spend time there working and fly back to Tofino. From 1987 to 1995, I worked with Frank O'Neill and his crew to change the look of Vancouver International Airport. It was a powerful time. I have heard it said many, many times that YVR is one of the most beautiful airports in the world.

The year 1987 was a big one for me as it was the year of the Commonwealth Heads of Government Meeting in Vancouver. Premier Vander Zalm chose a painting that I did, called *A Meeting of Chiefs* (p.43), to be presented to Queen Elizabeth II.

At this time, Eagle Aerie Gallery was very busy; we had hundreds of thousands of people visiting. I told stories to thousands of people. It was a most satisfying time because as an artist, I am a storyteller.

I created the Vancouver series following the Victoria series. My most popular art piece is *Siwash Rock* (p.47), inspired by the book *Legends of Vancouver* by E. Pauline Johnson. I placed a portrait of my friend Chief Dan George in the painting as he was another great teacher of mine. I became an actor for a brief time and did two episodes of *The Beachcombers* in Gibsons, BC. One of the great lessons that Dan George taught me was that I should always speak from my heart. He said, "When you speak from your mind, only their minds hear you. When we get old sometimes, we forget. When we speak from our heart, people's hearts hear us, and our hearts never forget."

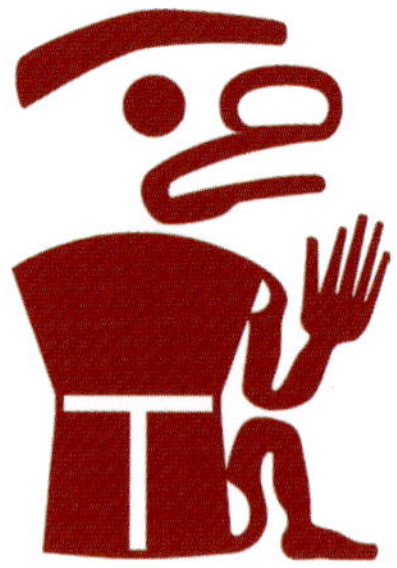

In 1992, the architects and designers invited me to be artistic adviser to the board of Saanich Commonwealth Place. It was a wonderful, wonderful project. A great part of that project was my first large totem, the ten-metre Salmon Totem I carved in Tofino. In 1994 the Commonwealth Games were held in Victoria and Queen Elizabeth II walked through the doors of Saanich Commonwealth Place at a special ceremony there. I felt like I was progressing well as an artist.

That same year, 1994, I was chosen as one of thirteen extraordinary Canadian achievers to be on the Honour Roll of *Maclean's* magazine. I was the first Canadian visual artist to be nominated. I met Peter C. Newman, who told me, "You are a visionary. I nominated you for the *Maclean's* award."

The greatest honour in my life was my adoption into the House of Walkus by Dorothy Walkus. Dorothy's son, Ted Walkus, is Hosumdas, the head chief of the House of Walkus. I was dressed in regalia by chiefs and from that day on I became Tlakwagila from the House of Walkus. Tlakwa is the word for copper and Gila is man—Copperman is the literal translation of Tlakwagila. I went to Nuwagawa, my Auntie Evelyn, and asked about the name Tlakwagila. She smiled and said, "You go to Rivers Inlet and you get Ted to show you the painting on the rock. That place is called Tlakwagila; that's where your name comes from. It means, 'He wears a copper on his back.'" When you look at the painting, it looks like the copper is a person, a head, arms and legs. She said, "It also means, 'He makes coppers.' Those are the translations of Tlakwagila: copper maker, copper owner or he is a copper."

In 1998, I got the news that I was going to receive the Order of British Columbia for my work as an artist and Indigenous leader in British Columbia. Two of Mr. West's students from Oak Bay High School have received the Order of BC, Carole Sabiston and me. Mr. West was an exceptional art teacher and remained my friend to the end of his life.

In 2003 it was a wonderful experience to work on my second art book, *Copperman*. I increased the size of the book and proofed all the colours and the images. *Copperman* was released by my company, Eagle Dancer Enterprises. So it was that I gained the title of publisher.

In 2004, my family and I found a beautiful piece of property in Hazelton, and I moved

Roy's *Tlakwagila* design was inspired by Wuikinuxv First Nation art painted on a rock at Rivers Inlet on BC's central coast.

back to the town where I spent so much time as a child and fell in love with horses and went to art school. Three years after moving to Hazelton, in 2007, I was notified that I was to become a Member of the Order of Canada. Life continued to be busy and exciting with horses. We are members of the Kispiox Valley Rodeo Association; horses and ranchers are part of our community.

In my meetings with different people, I kept talking about a magazine that was published out of the BC Provincial Museum when I was living in Victoria. The one particular story I enjoyed was called *Paddlewheels on the Frontier*; it reminded me how special Hazelton was in the Skeena Valley. The magazine came with cassette tapes of Imbert Orchard interviewing people that I knew in Hazelton. I was living back in Hazelton and was telling people about a story of the old name for the Skeena. On the tapes, I heard Imbert Orchard ask Chief Johnson of Kispiox, "What is the actual name of the Skeena River?" Chief Johnson told him the story of how he had asked so many different people and wasn't satisfied with the answers. Finally, he asked this old lady in Kitwanga, and it just so happened that that old lady was from Kitkatla. He asked her, "Do you know the old name of the Skeena River?" And she told him, "Yes, Ksan." Chief Johnson said, "Yes, the name of the river is Ksan and the people who live along that river are Git, our word for people. Gitksan actually means people of that river." I loved to be back in Hazelton telling this story, and I tried to find the recording so I could let them hear it, but I couldn't find it. Somebody told me about a man with a company called Memories to Memoirs. I found Robert "Lucky" Budd, who has listened to all Imbert Orchard's tapes at the Royal BC Museum. Lucky and I became friends. So, Lucky's here helping me put together this book, which is full of memoirs. So fitting that we're together doing this. Lucky introduced me to Harbour Publishing and we now have a list of many books.

Lucky came to Tofino to listen to storytelling at the gallery and stayed for four days and recorded storytelling sessions. I realized that people coming to the gallery wanted to hear the stories of inspiration behind the art. Lucky came to me after recording one day and said, "Roy, you have books here." I said, "Stories are meant to be told." Lucky responded with, "Yes, but you will teach thousands of people if you put them in books." Our first book was called *Raven Brings the Light* and it came out in 2013, and the next year Harbour published my third art book, *Storyteller*.

Speaking of storytelling, every time I would visit Vancouver I met with my brother Ted Walkus, who lives in Ladner. One day

Ted and I went to the Museum of Anthropology at UBC because I wanted to show him my favourite totem. We walked up to this totem and he said, "Wow, you know why you always used to come to this totem? Because you are Tlakwagila, you are the grandson of the man who had this totem carved, the chief who had this totem carved." I looked at him with disbelief and thought, *Ah, he's telling me a joke here*. I asked, "What do you mean, Ted?" He said, "That totem was stolen from our family in Owikeeno. It belongs in front of the Big House of Auntie Evelyn." I broke down in tears. It was one of those feelings like, *I'm part of a story and the story is old. All of the choices that I've made in my life have kept me going in the story. I can see how it's unfolded by observing different things that happened*. When I heard Ted's words—"that totem was stolen from our family"—I realized that with my knowledge as an artist, one of the greatest things that I could do would be to return that totem to my Auntie Evelyn and have it raised in Owikeeno. I said, "Ted, I want to get all the photographs of that totem I can. I want to re-carve that totem and put it back in Owikeeno," and he agreed.

Many people came together: the owner of Good Hope Cannery, Tony Allard; Sid Keay from Duncanby Lodge and many, many more helped make that totem a possibility. My brother Ted and I stood by the giant cedar tree near Owikeeno and sang a journeying song. We stopped singing in the middle of the song and Ted said, "We will finish the song when this tree becomes a totem and is raised in our village." So it is that the Hosumdas Totem was completed and raised in 2018.

The year 2018 was also when I completed work on the Grateful Dead's *Pacific Northwest* box set. It was nominated for a Grammy Award for Best Boxed or Special Limited Edition Package, the one and only time a Canadian visual artist was ever nominated for a Grammy. This is the story.

Lucky Budd called me one day and asked, "Are you interested in doing something for the Grateful Dead? A box set of CDs?" I went to Victoria to meet with Lucky and David Lemieux, the archivist for the Grateful Dead, and the groundwork for designing a boxed set of CDs began. *Grateful Dead* (p. 91) is one of the designs on the box. I loved working with the Rhino record executives. Once again it seemed so much a part of a life unfolding like a book; you turn the blank page and a story appears. Music, which has been such a big part of my life, guided me to this place. I remember one of the Rhino team members saying, "Could you talk to us a little more about your ideas for this Grateful Dead package?" I told them about the gift of a song from a traditional singer and composer that was

UBC (1988) is from Roy's Vancouver series. With a 1977 show titled *Beginnings*, Roy was the first of many Indigenous artists to have a one-person exhibition at the Museum of Anthropology at UBC.

given to me as Tlakwagila. William Wasden, the writer/singer, gave me the song and said, "This song is for Tlakwagila to put in his treasure box."

In our traditional ways on the Northwest Coast, we speak of standing in the strength of who we are, to lead in a good way. When we do our duty as leaders, our ancestors on the other side are excitedly whispering to each other, "Maybe this will be the one who brings forth the strength, truth and beauty in our lineage; they are the grateful dead." When I stopped talking to the Rhino team, there was silence. I immediately thought, *Oh, they didn't like that*. I asked, "Is everybody there?" One of them said, "Oh yes, we're all sitting at the table in tears. Roy, whatever you want do for this box set, you do it." I knew at that moment it was going to be the Grateful Dead's treasure chest. That treasure chest was nominated for a Grammy.

I have enjoyed a few years on the BC Arts Council and appreciate a new friend and brother, Stan Chung. Stan knew I was getting on in life, close to being eighty years old, and suggested that I be nominated as the first Elder-in-Residence to the BC Arts Council. My artistic life continues as Elder-in-Residence to the BC Arts Council.

This elder artist has always loved teaching, and I will continue to teach creatively.

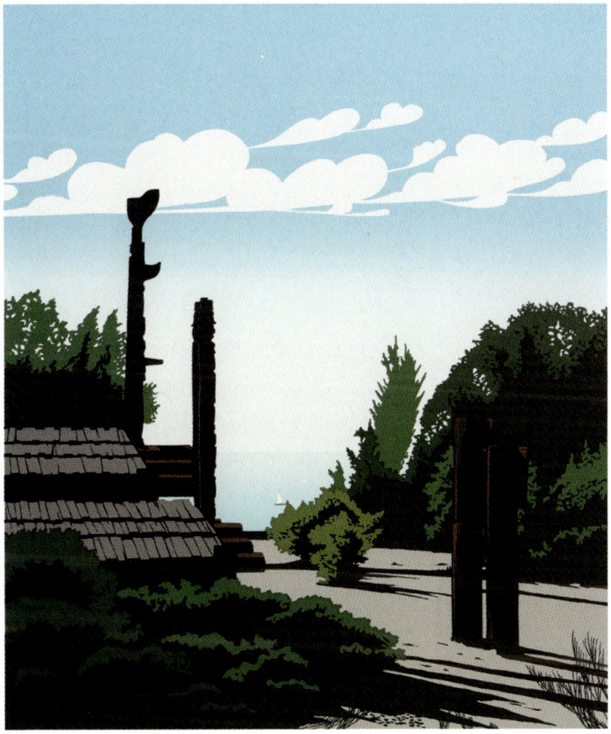

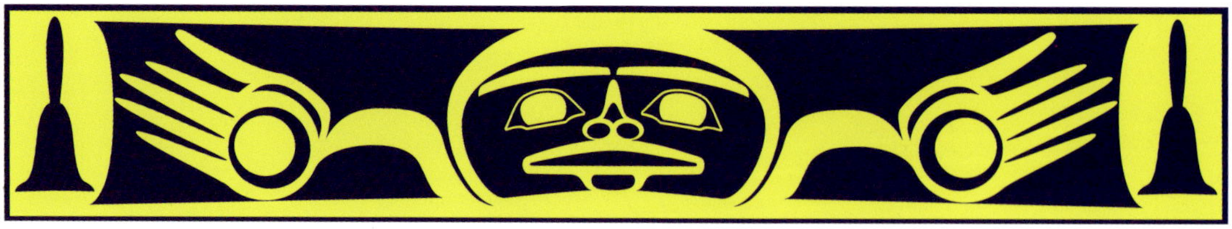

The Four Directions

THESE ARE TEACHINGS that are shared by people all around the world. These teachings have come to be known as the Four Directions.

We are all teachers, healers, visionaries and leaders.

As teachers, we keep our eyes, ears and hearts open to the lessons available to us each day, and these lessons become part of what we teach.

As healers, we pay attention to matters of the heart: our emotions, our healing journey becomes a healing journey of others. The world needs people who make decisions that will bring healing.

As visionaries, we come to see with our eyes closed. We can use this vision to see what needs to be done as teachers and healers.

We are all leaders. As leaders, we become more in tune with the truth of what is needed. We are all called to stand in our strength, truth and beauty and lead in a good way.

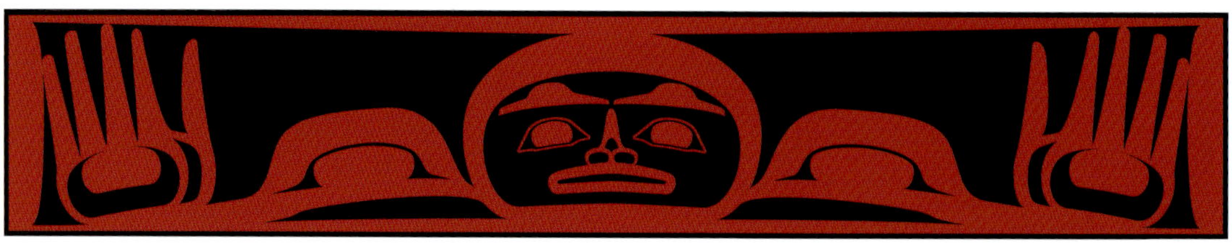

Sweat Lodge series (2009/2010). Top, *The Teacher*; above, *The Healer*; opposite top, *The Visionary*; opposite bottom, *The Leader.*

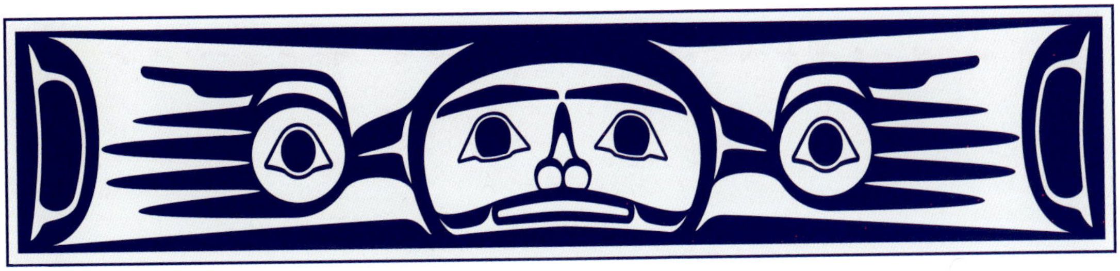

I LOOK TO THE EAST, the way of the teacher. I hear the instrument of the teacher, the bell. I ask that my eyes, ears and heart be open to the lessons that are available to me. The element is fire, and the colour is yellow. The sun is the daily fire that brings light to the world. As a teacher, the light is knowledge. The season of the teacher is spring. The human face is the face of a child. We are all children of the Earth. May I always have the heart of the child to help educate other children with the knowledge given to me.

I LOOK TO THE SOUTH, the way of the healer. I ask that my heart be open to my healing journey. Healing gives meaning to the lessons of the teacher. Our healing journey becomes a healing journey of others. The element of the healer is earth. The instrument is the drum. The colour is red. The human face of the healer is a woman and the season is summer. I'm thankful to Mother Earth for the food and medicine she provides.

I LOOK TO THE WEST, the way of the visionary. I'm thankful for this gift of vision which helps me to see my life journey. I hear the beat of the click sticks, the oldest instrument used to keep our timing. The element is water and the colour is black. The human face is that of a man and the season is autumn. I ask that my vision be clear to help me see myself on my path.

I LOOK TO THE NORTH, the direction of the leader. The element is air. The colour is white. The instrument of the leader is the rattle, and the season is winter. The human face is the elder. I ask for the courage to stand in strength, truth and beauty, with all of my ancestors helping me. All leaders are warriors who stand against the adversity and lead in a good and loving way.

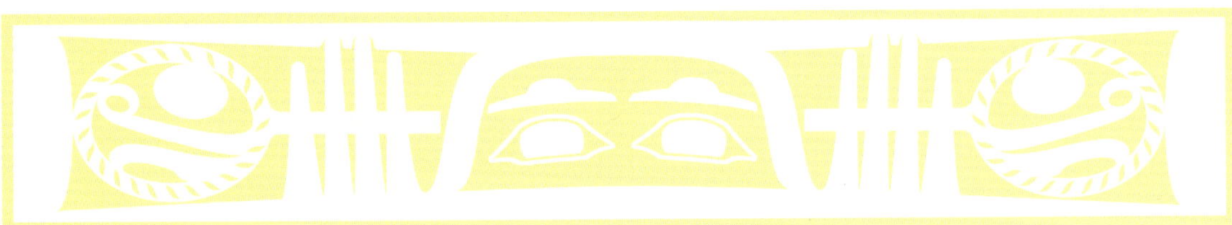

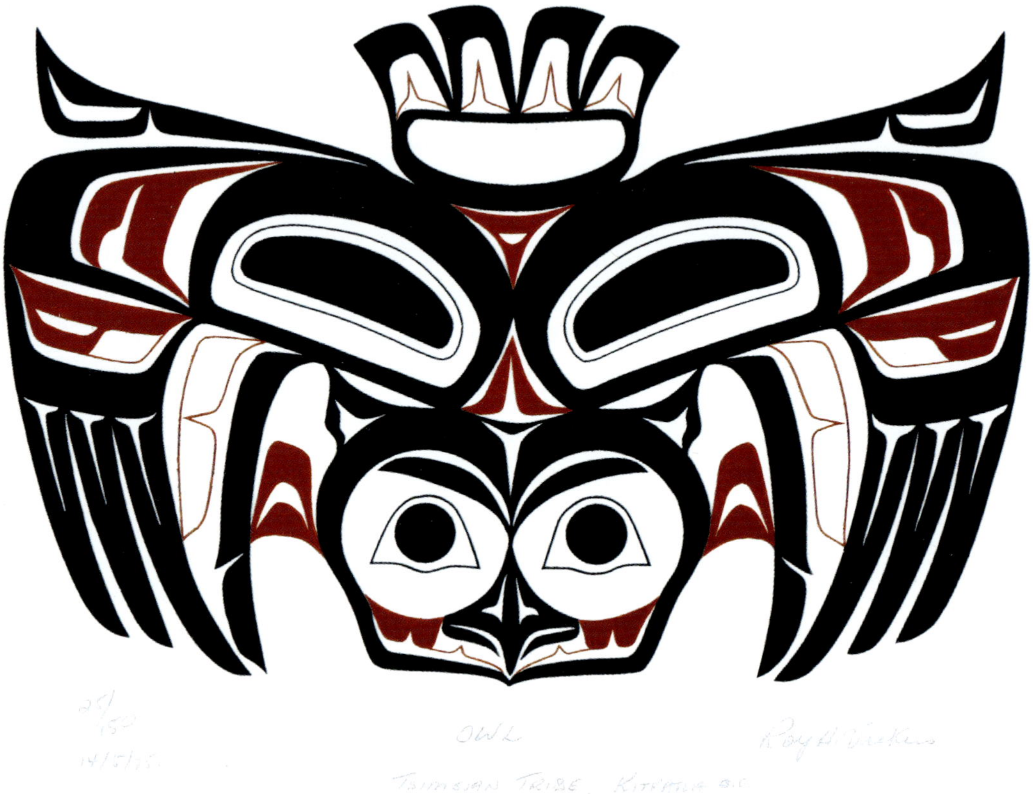

Owl 1975

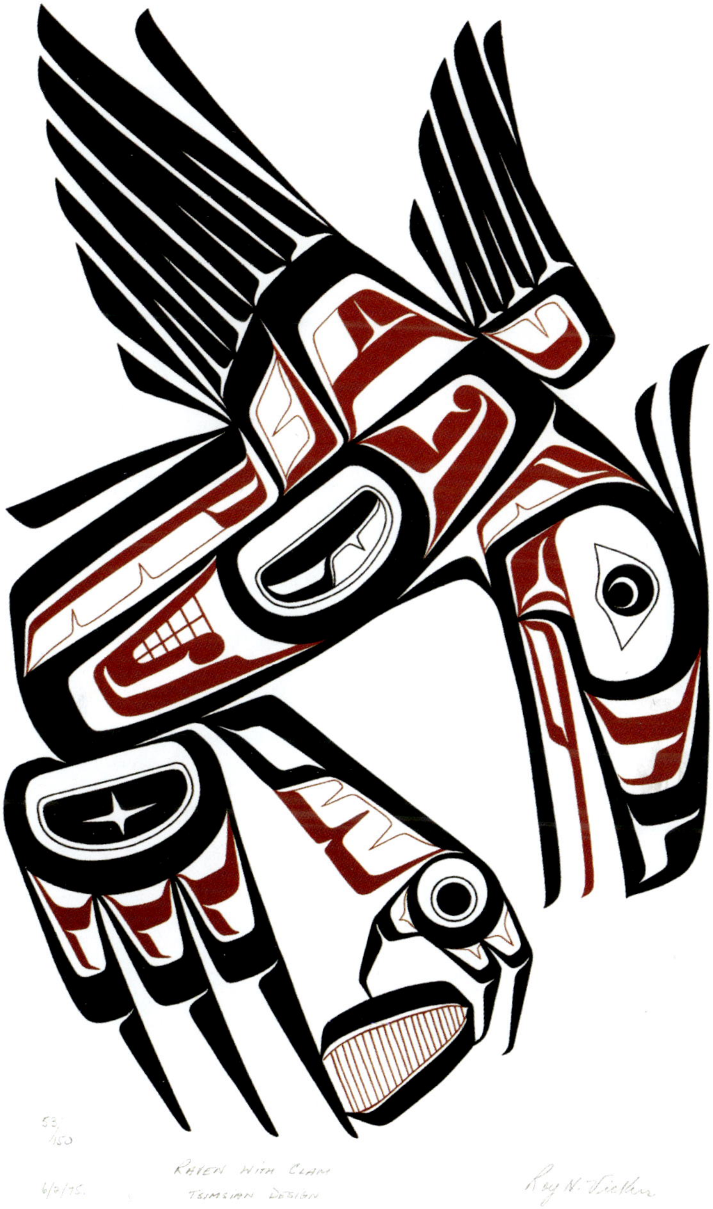

Raven with Clam 1975

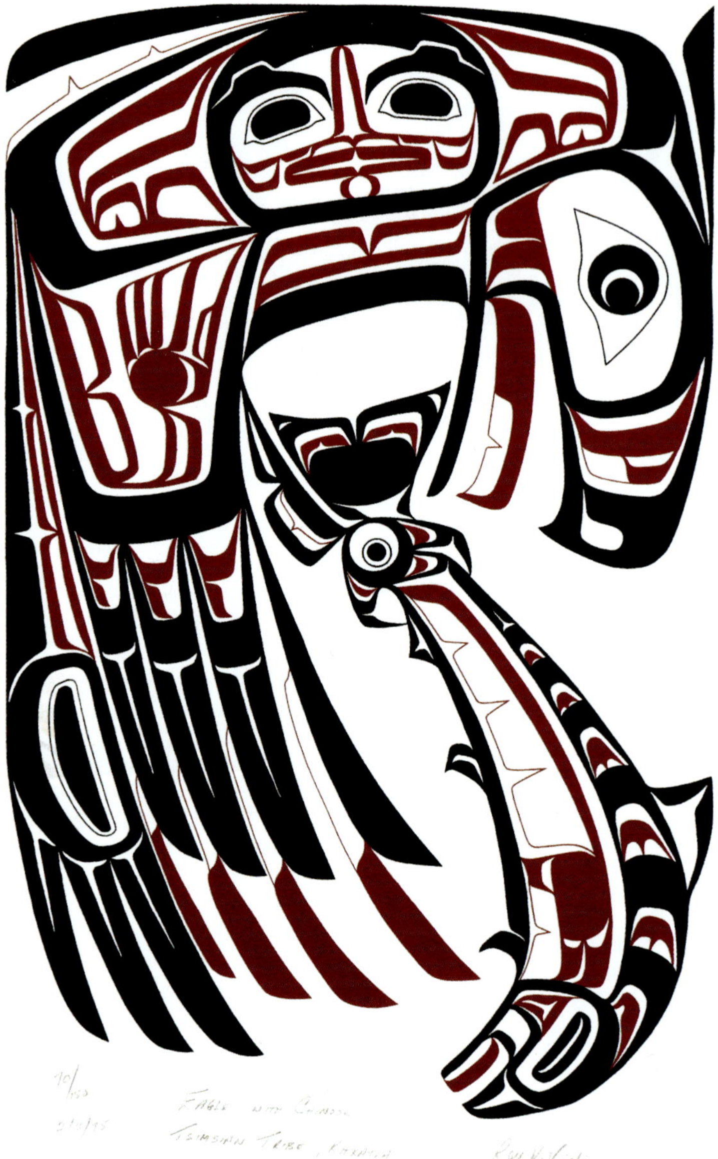

Eagle with Chinook 1975

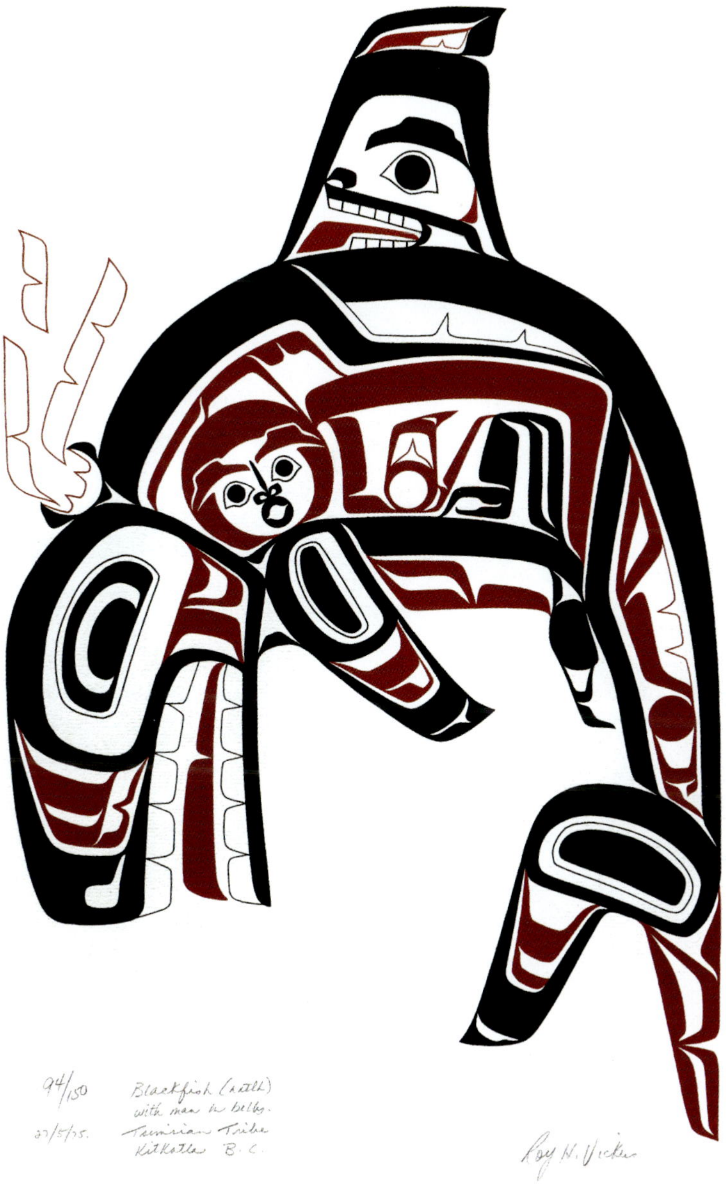

Blackfish 1975

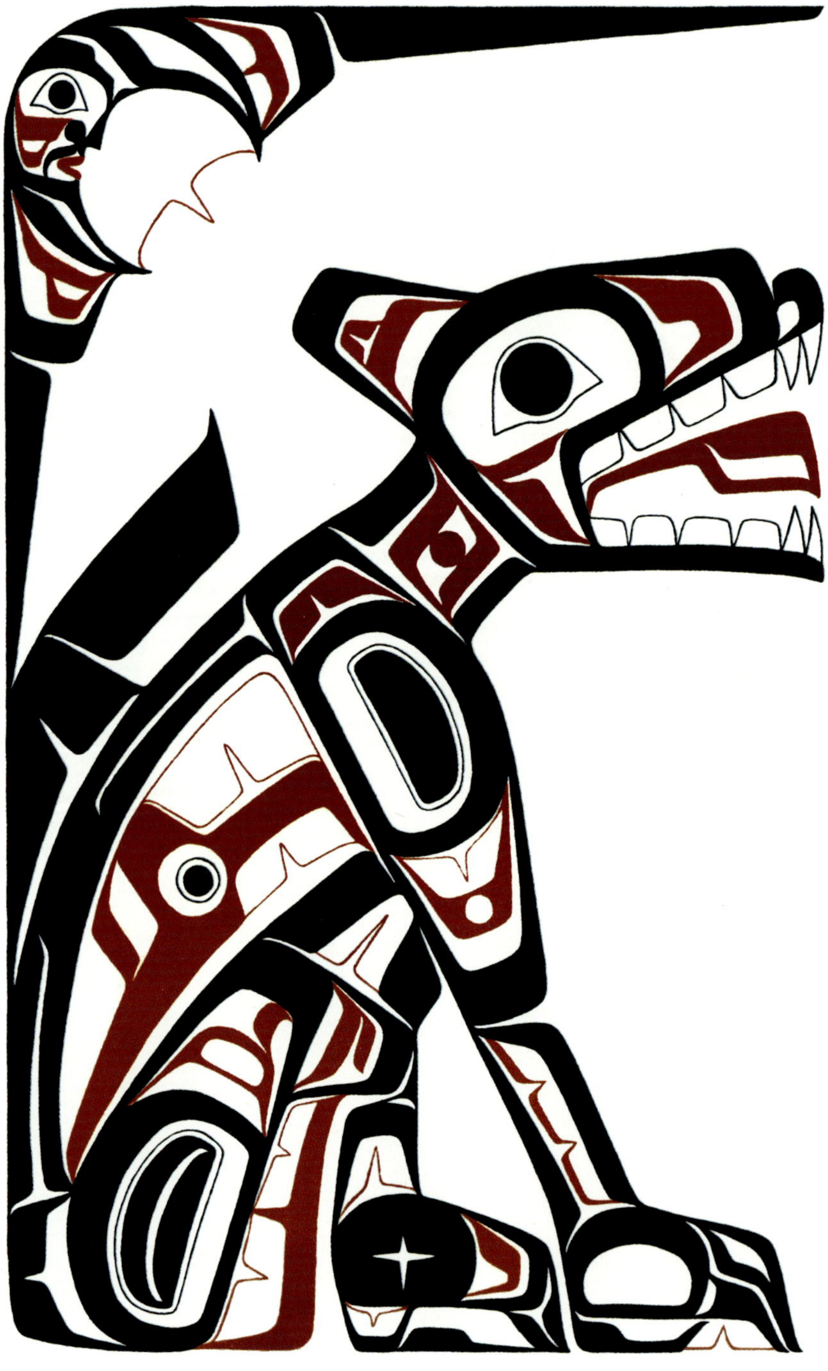
Roy H. Vickers
75

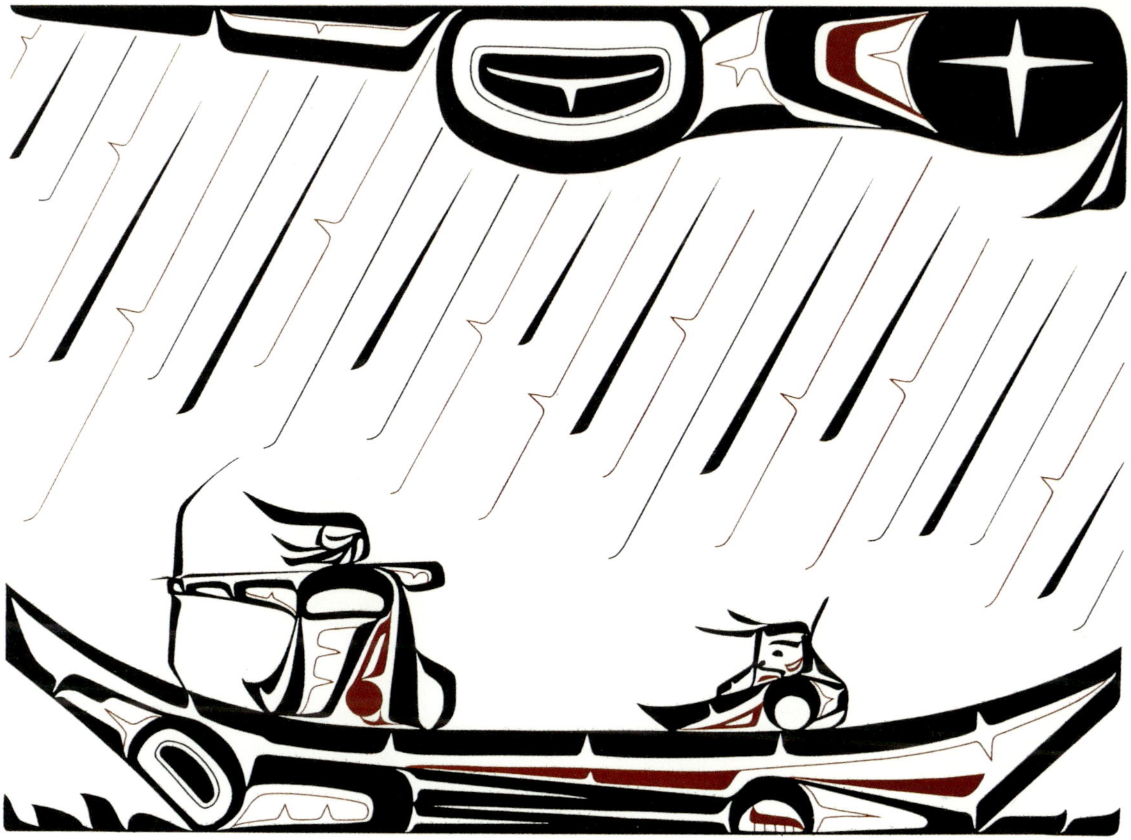

Wolf and Moon 1975 | *Oola! Oola!* 1976

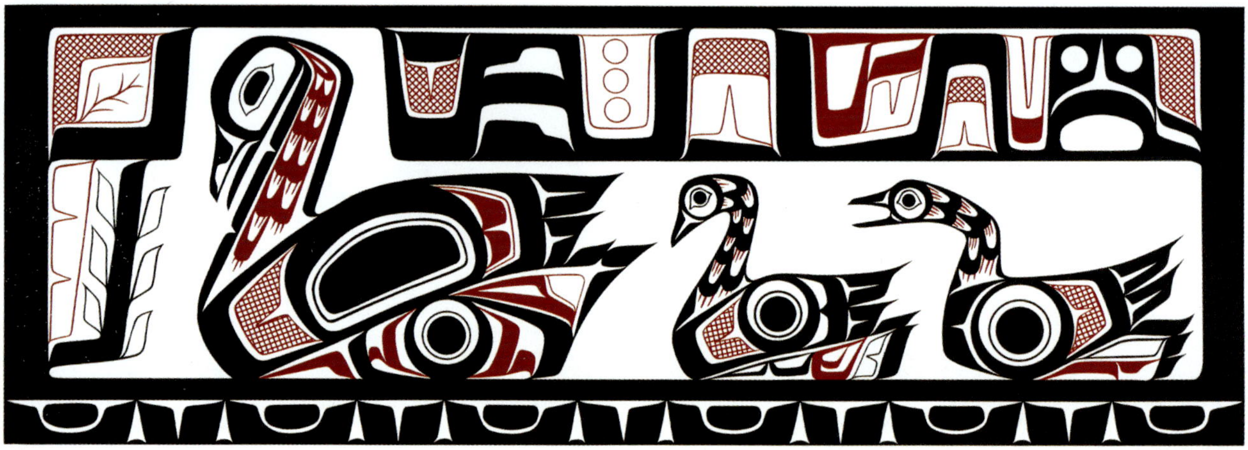

Stanley Park 1977

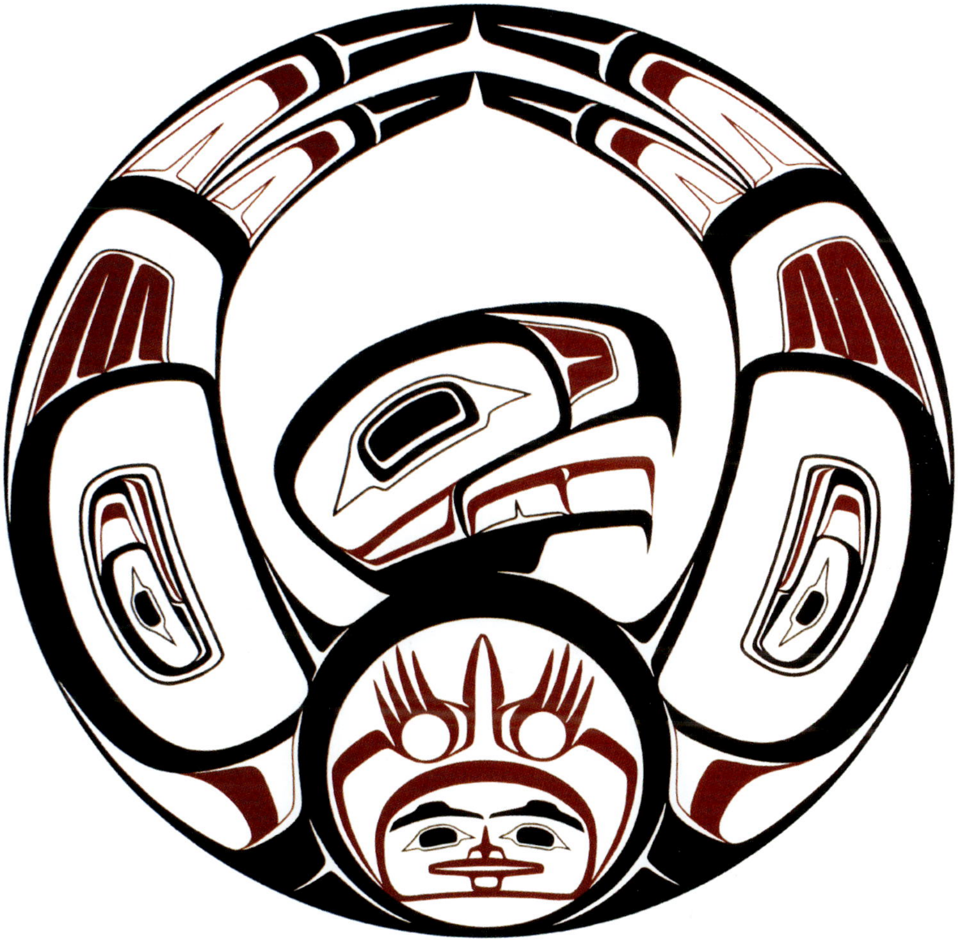

Eagle Full Circle 1982

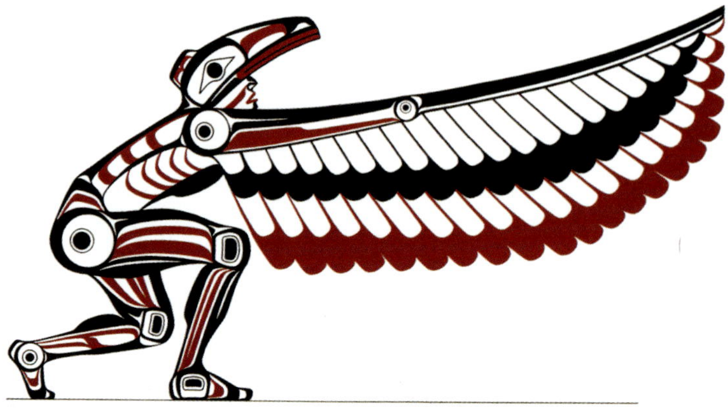

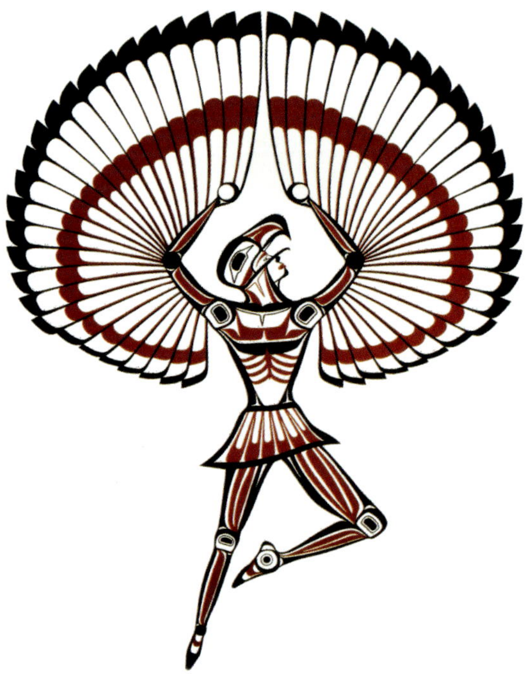

Ballet series: *Raven Dancer* 1982 | *Eagle Dancer II* 1982

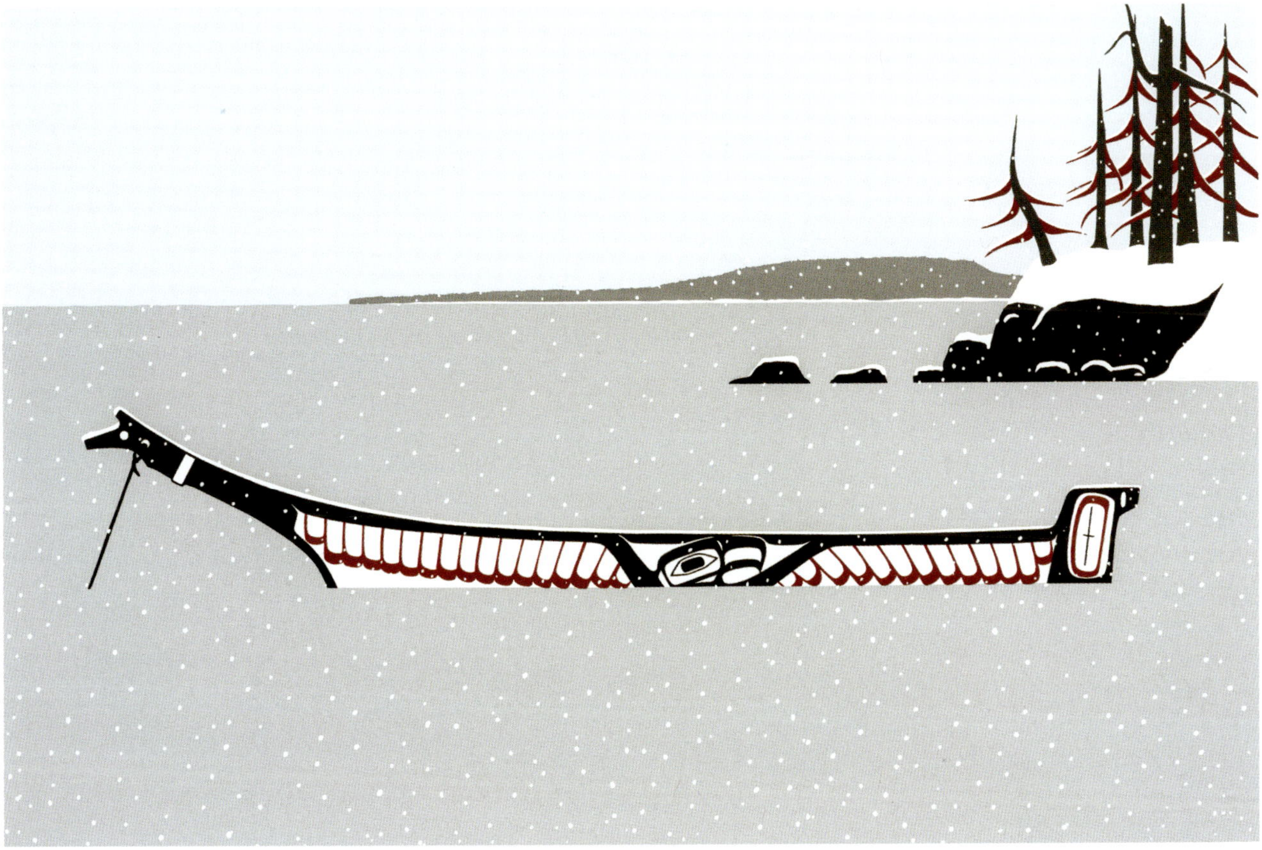

Canoe series: *Elegy* 1982

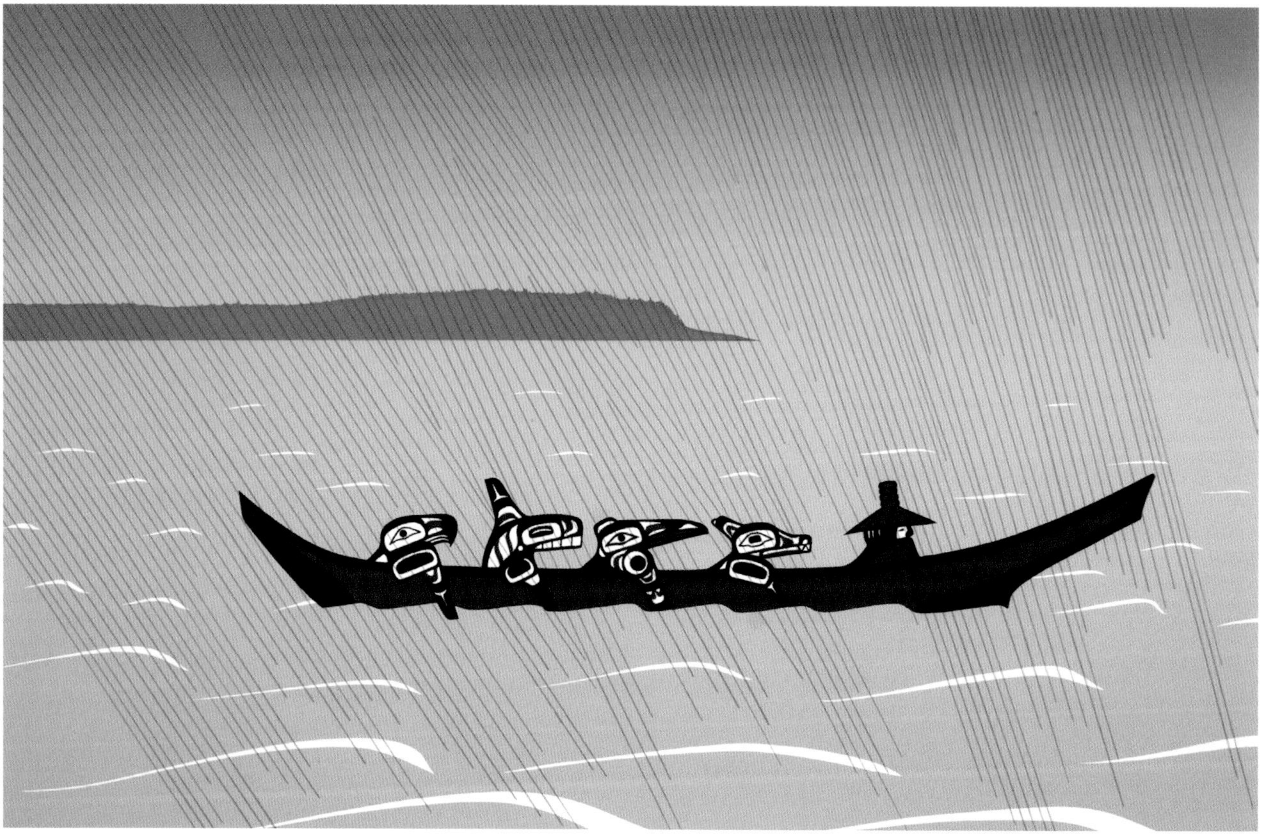

Canoe series: *Chief's Dream* 1982

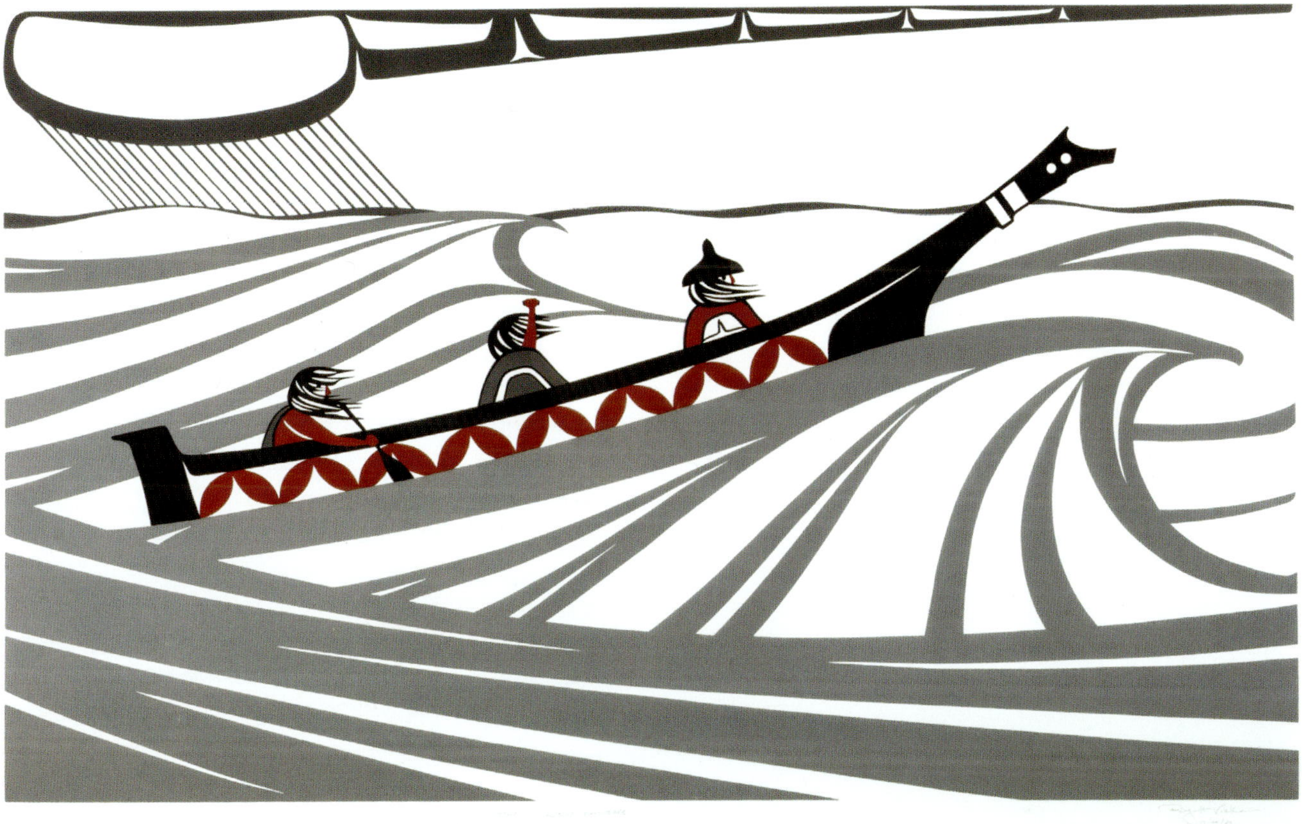

Canoe series: *The Westcoasters* 1982

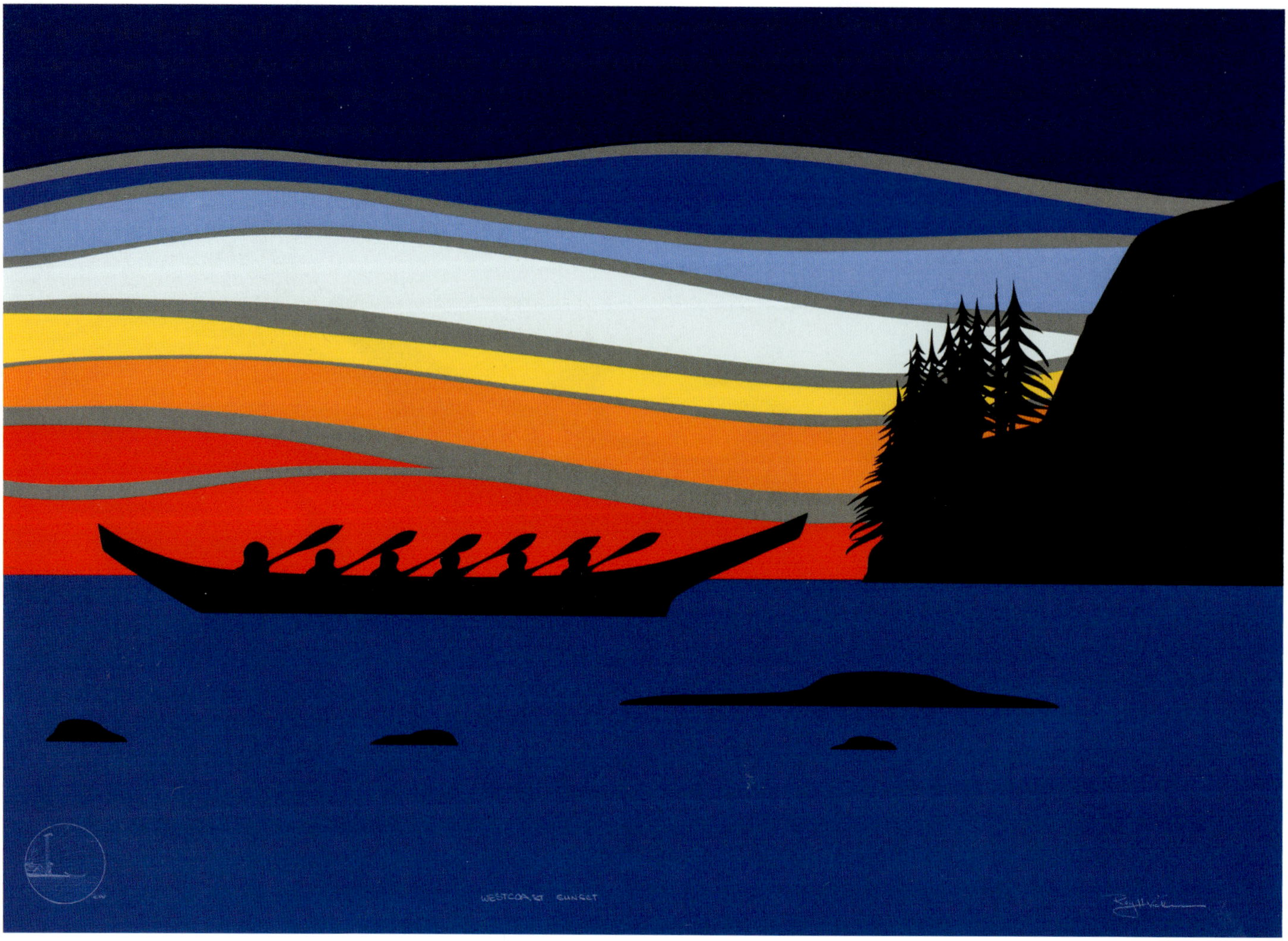

Canoe series: *Westcoast Sunset* 1982 | *Indian Summer* 1983

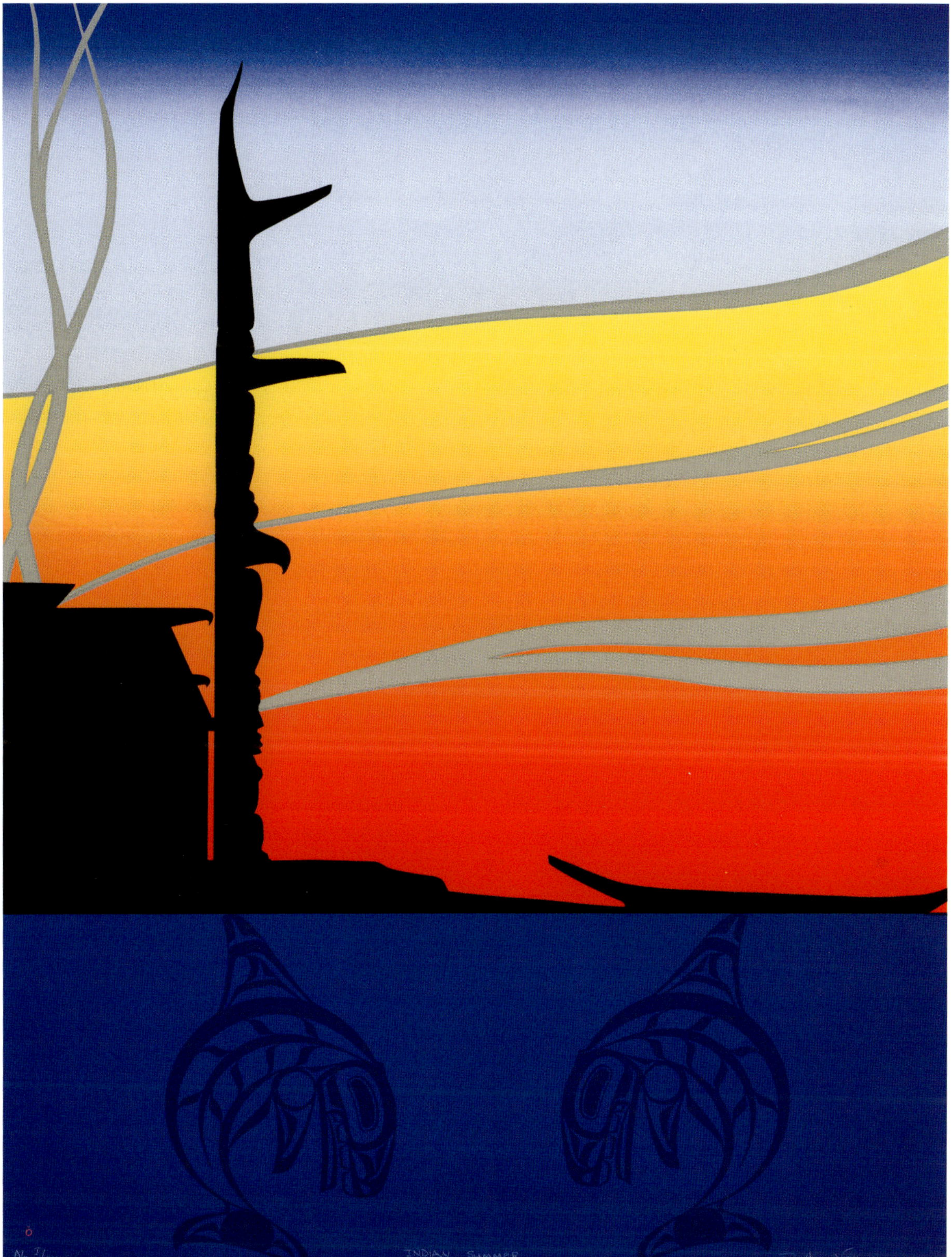
INDIAN SUMMER

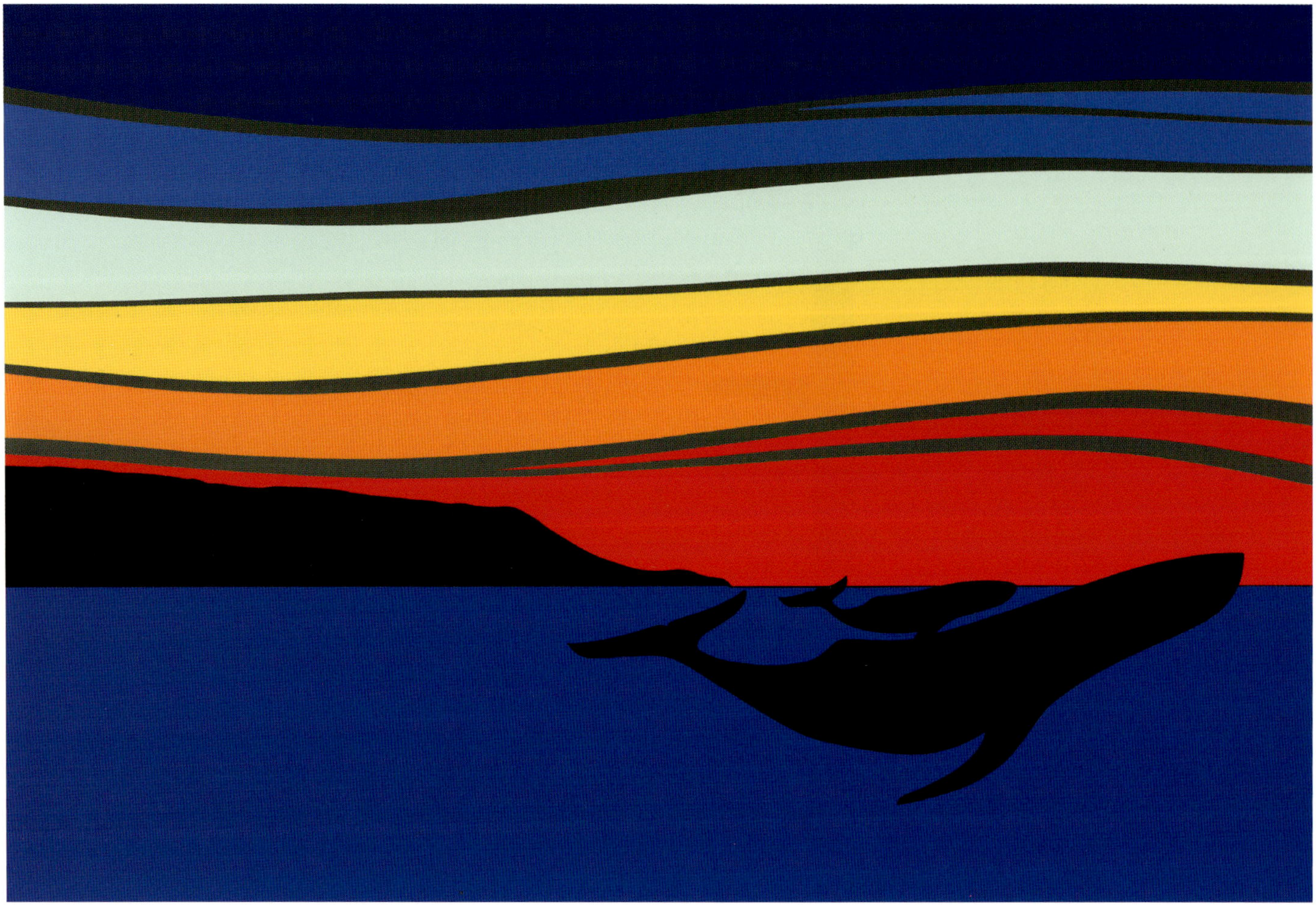

Pacific Sands 1983

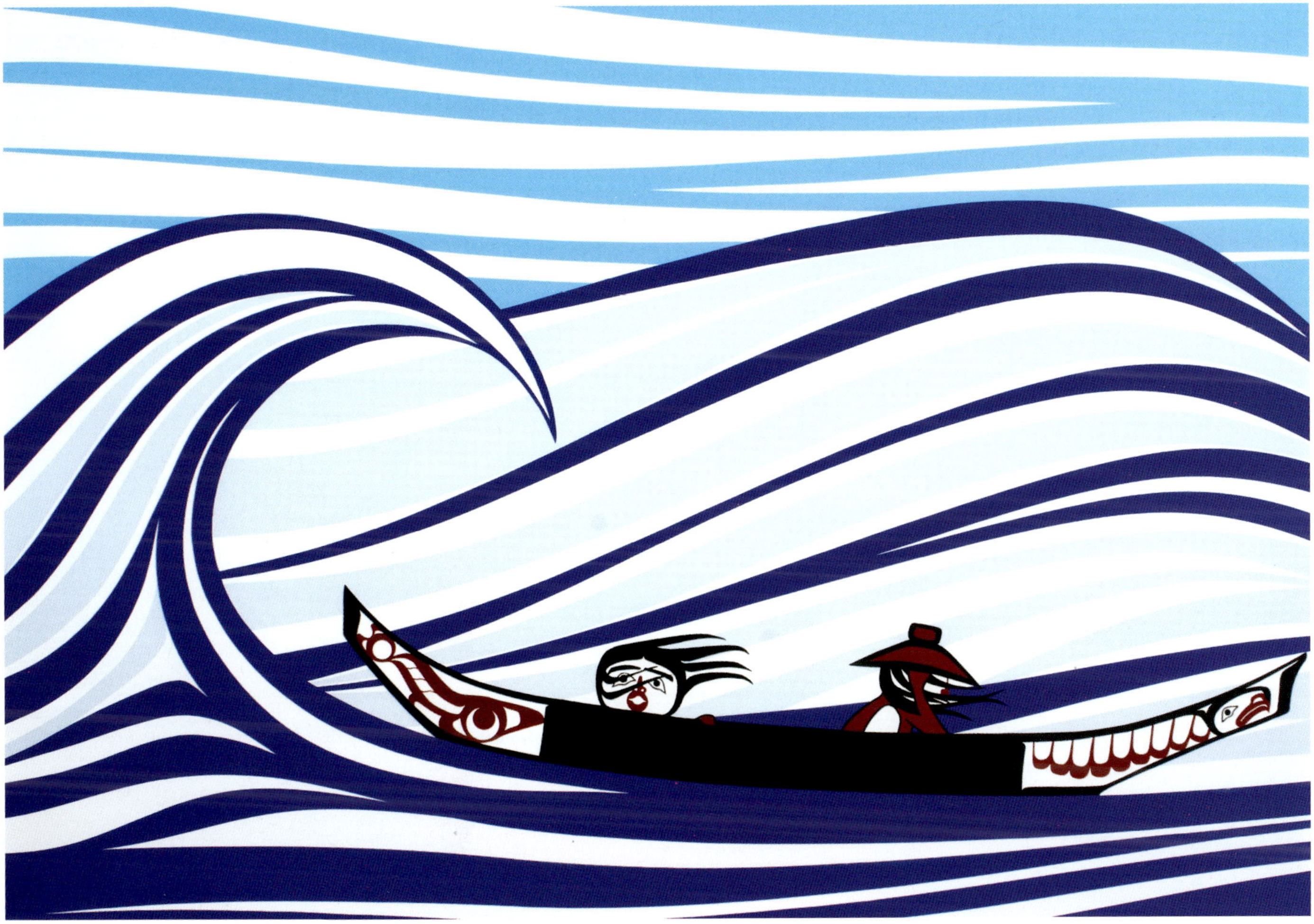

Goolka 1983

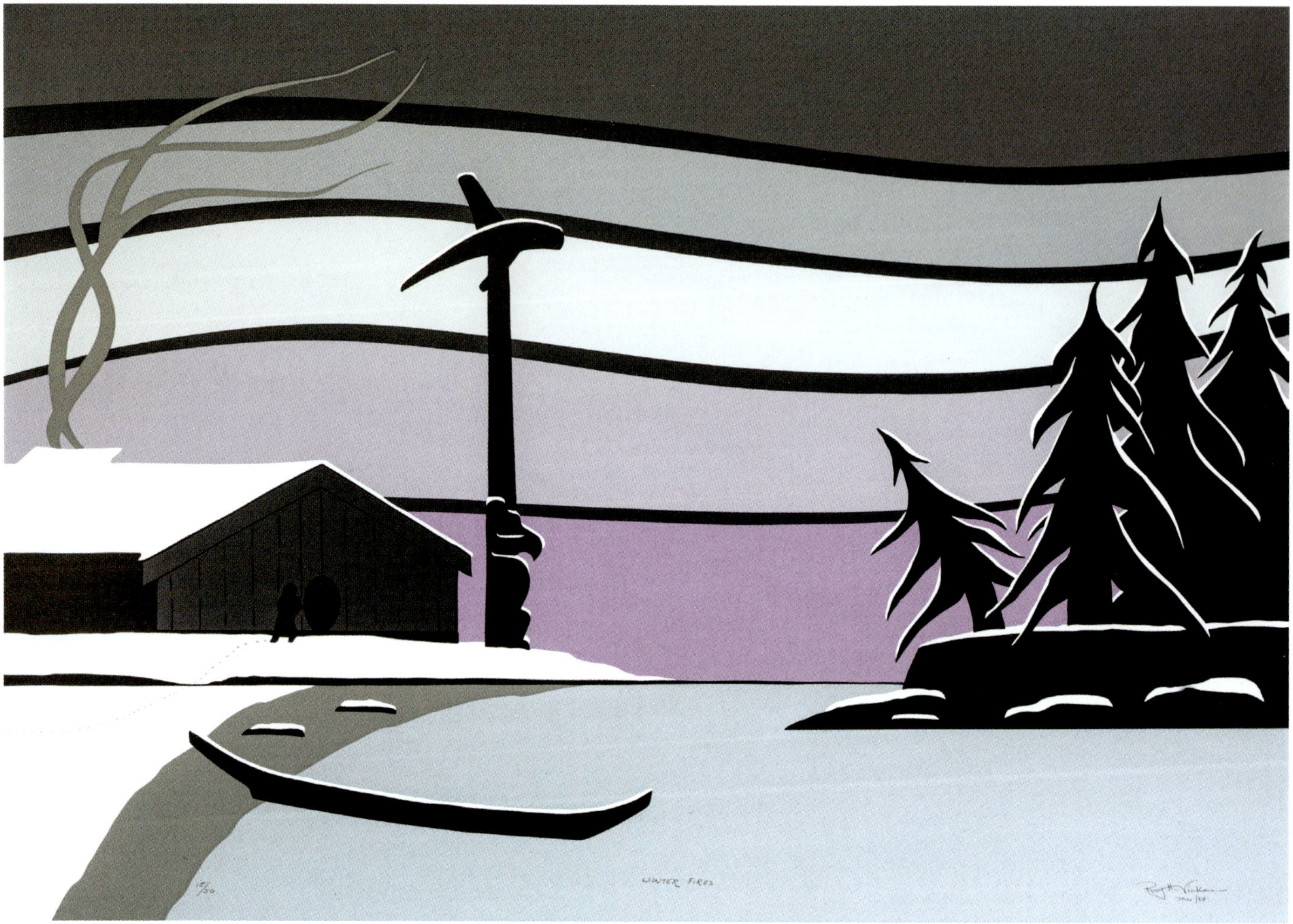

Winter Fires 1984

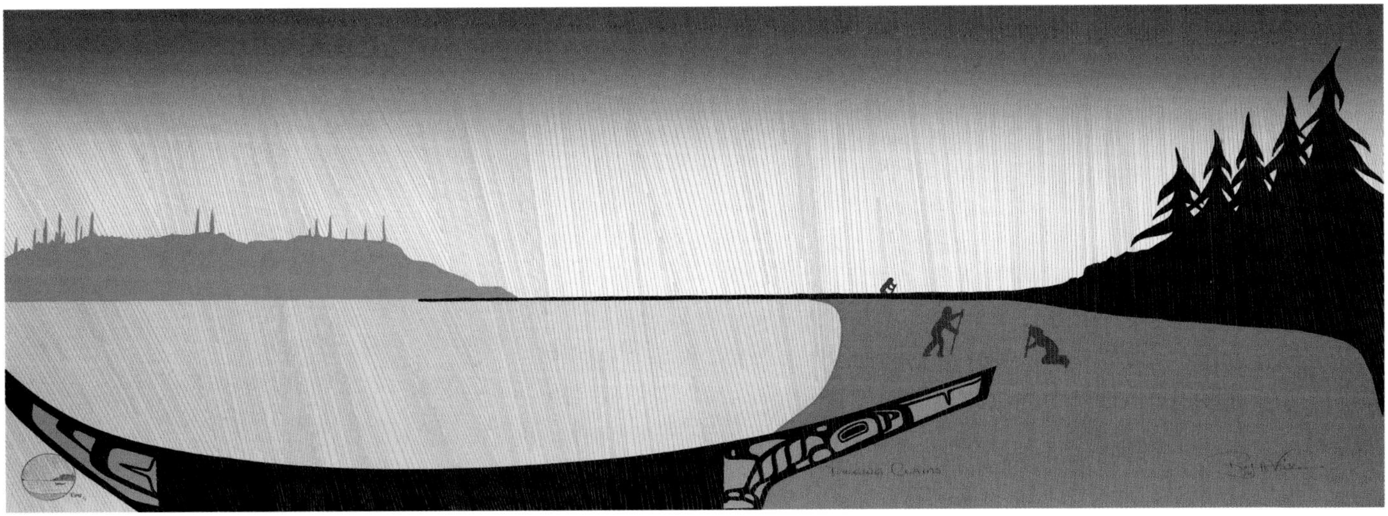

Digging Clams 1984

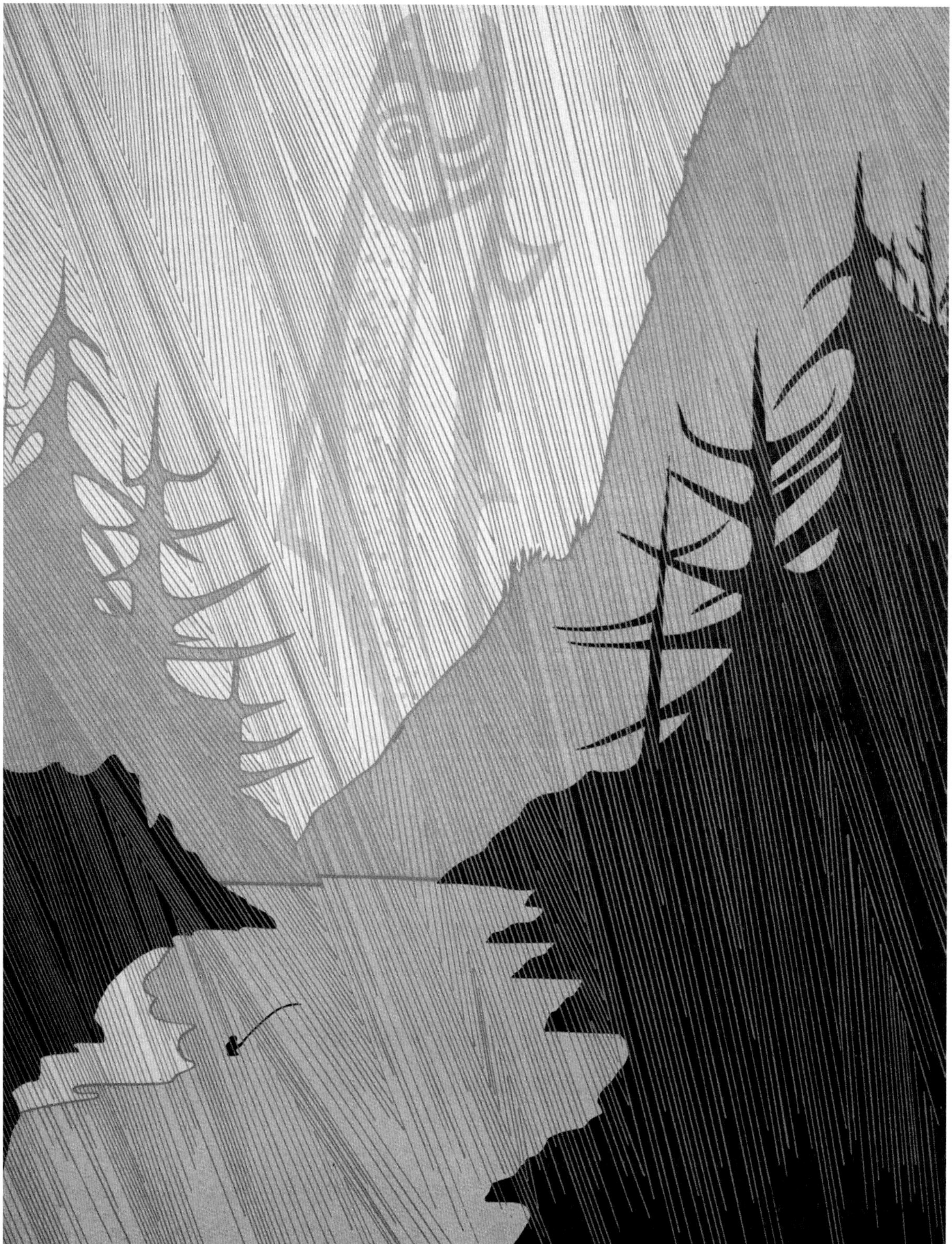

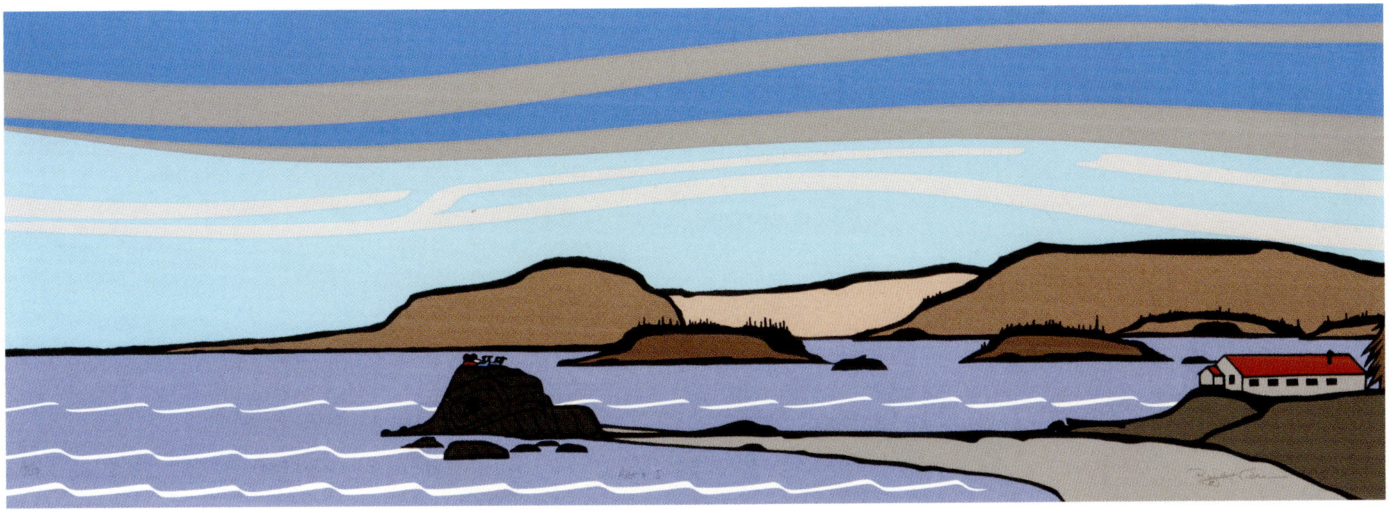

Steelhead 1984 | *Art & I* 1984

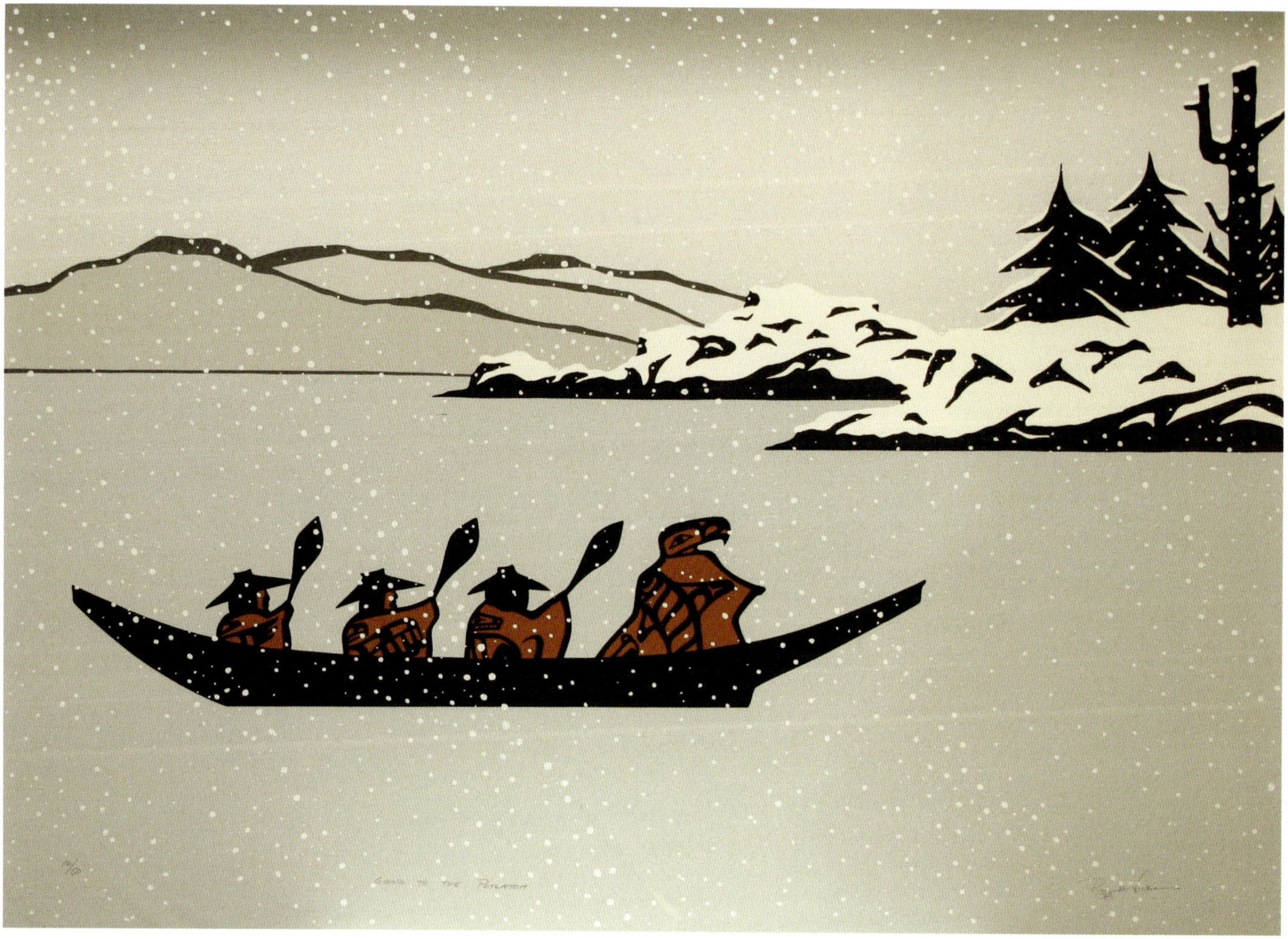

Going To The Potlatch 1984 | *Cypre River* 1985

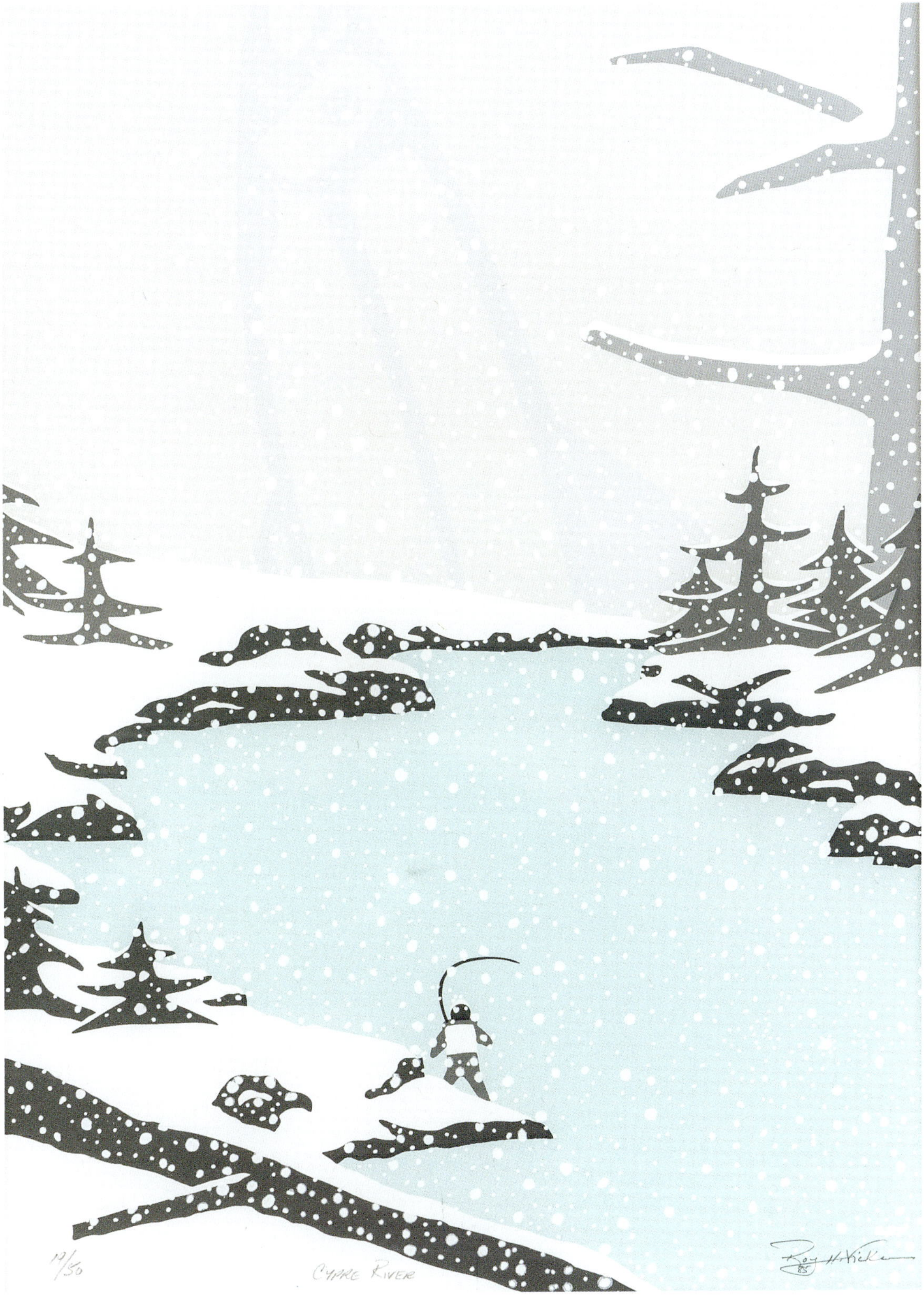

19/50
Cypre River
Roy H. Vickers
85

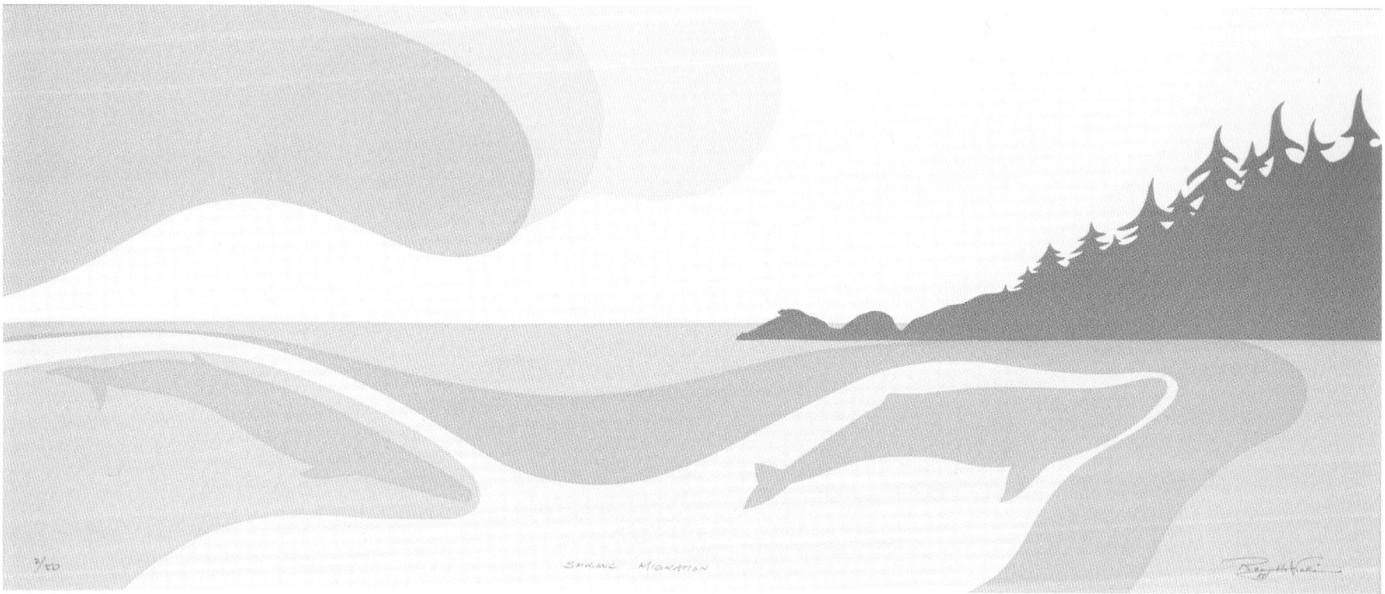

Spring Migration 1985

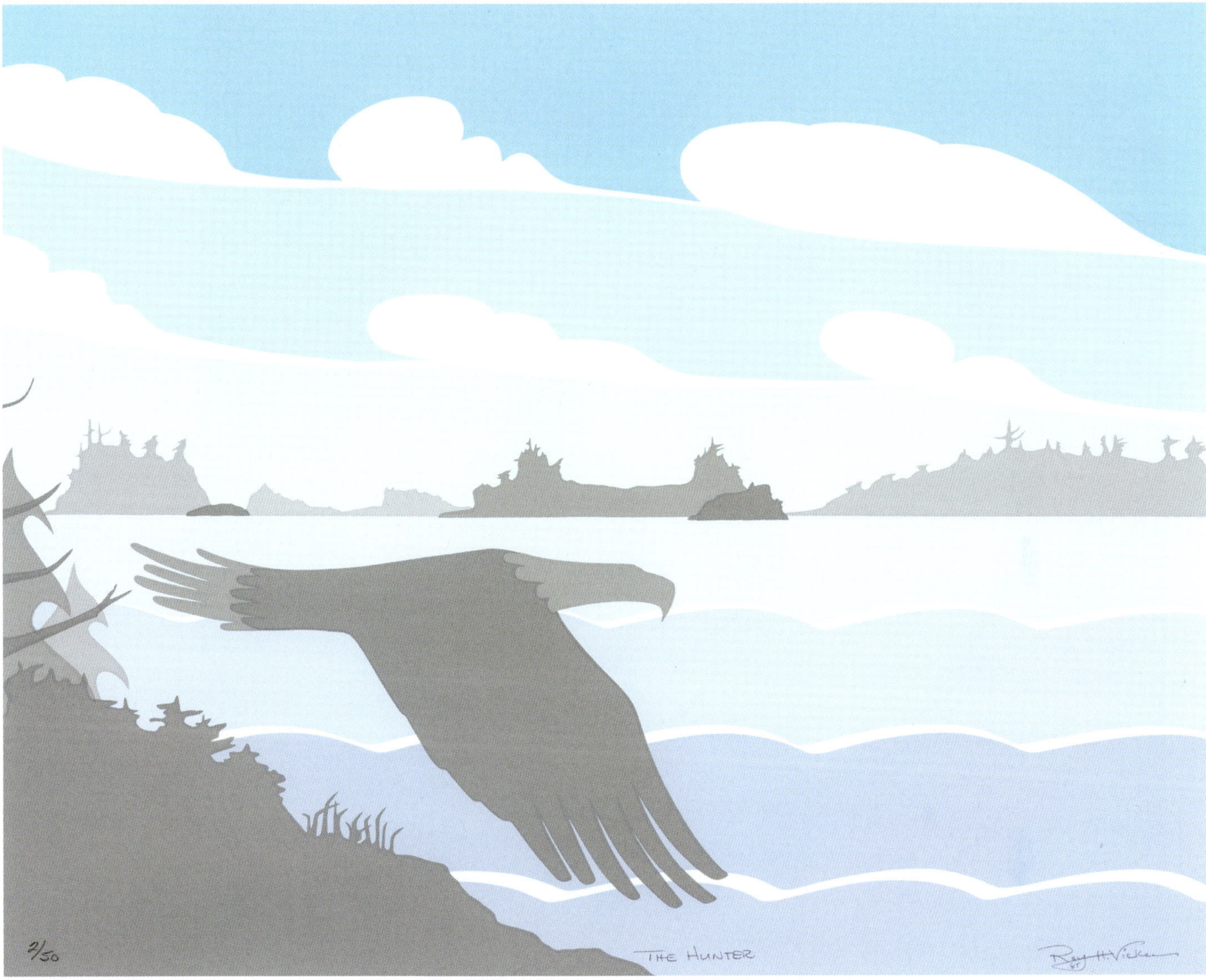

The Hunter 1985

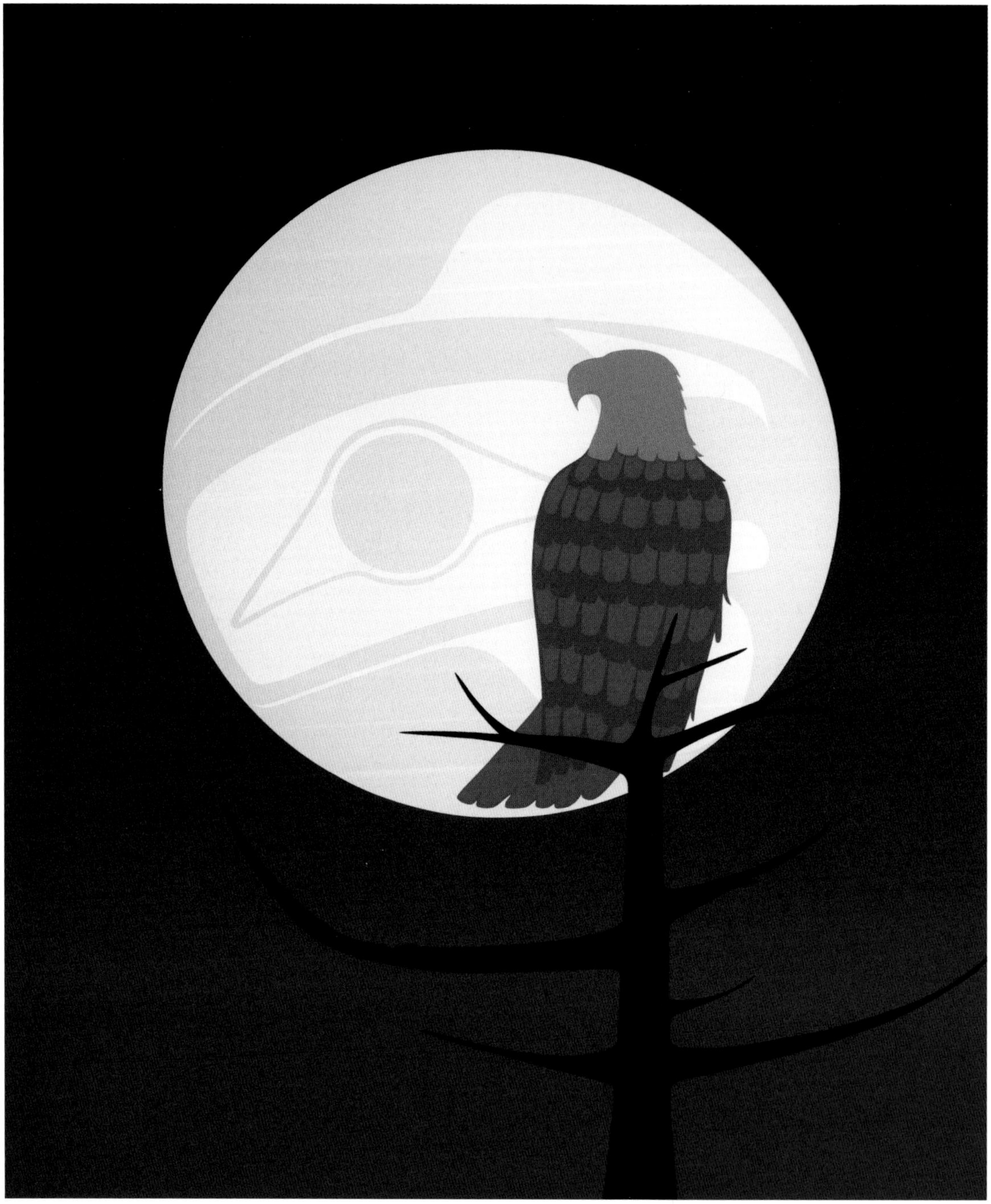

Eagle's Moon 1985

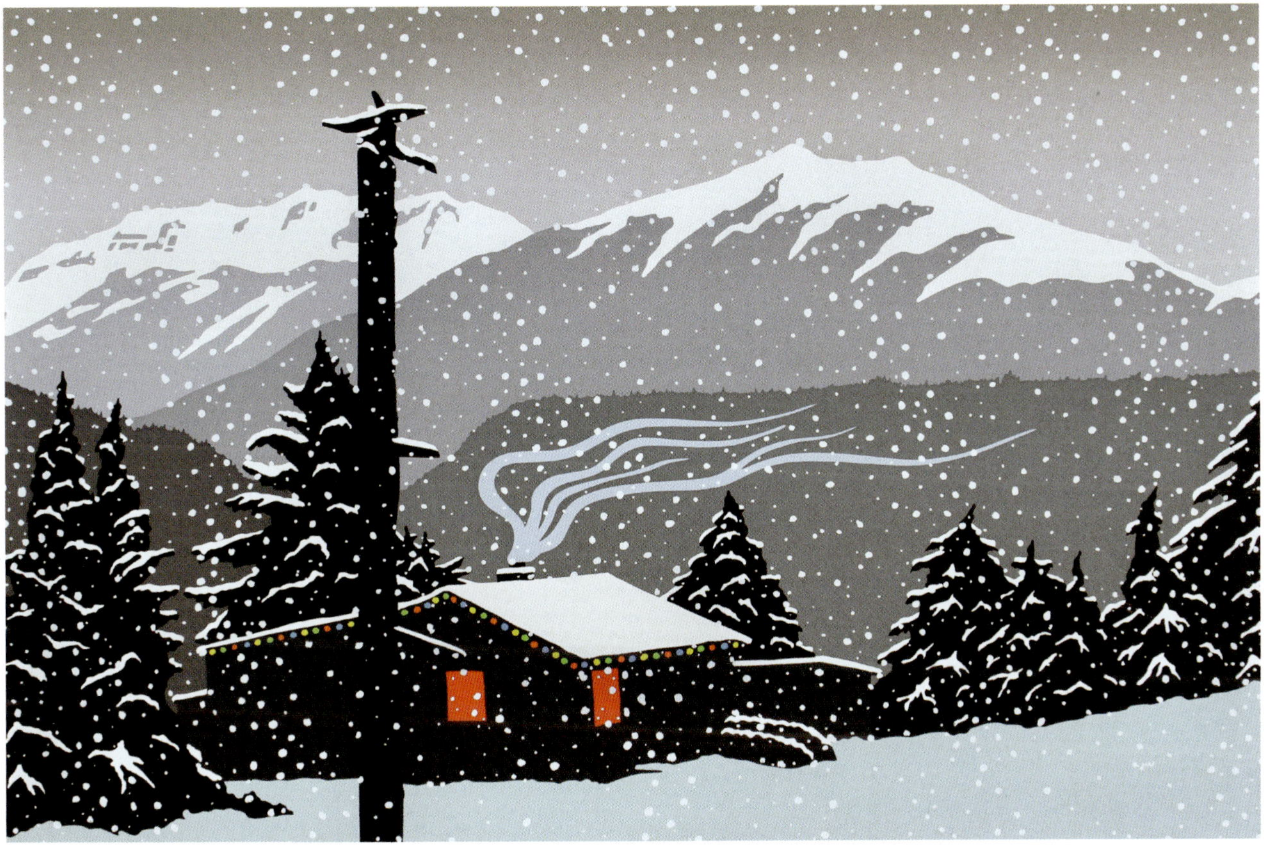

Skeena Crossing 1986

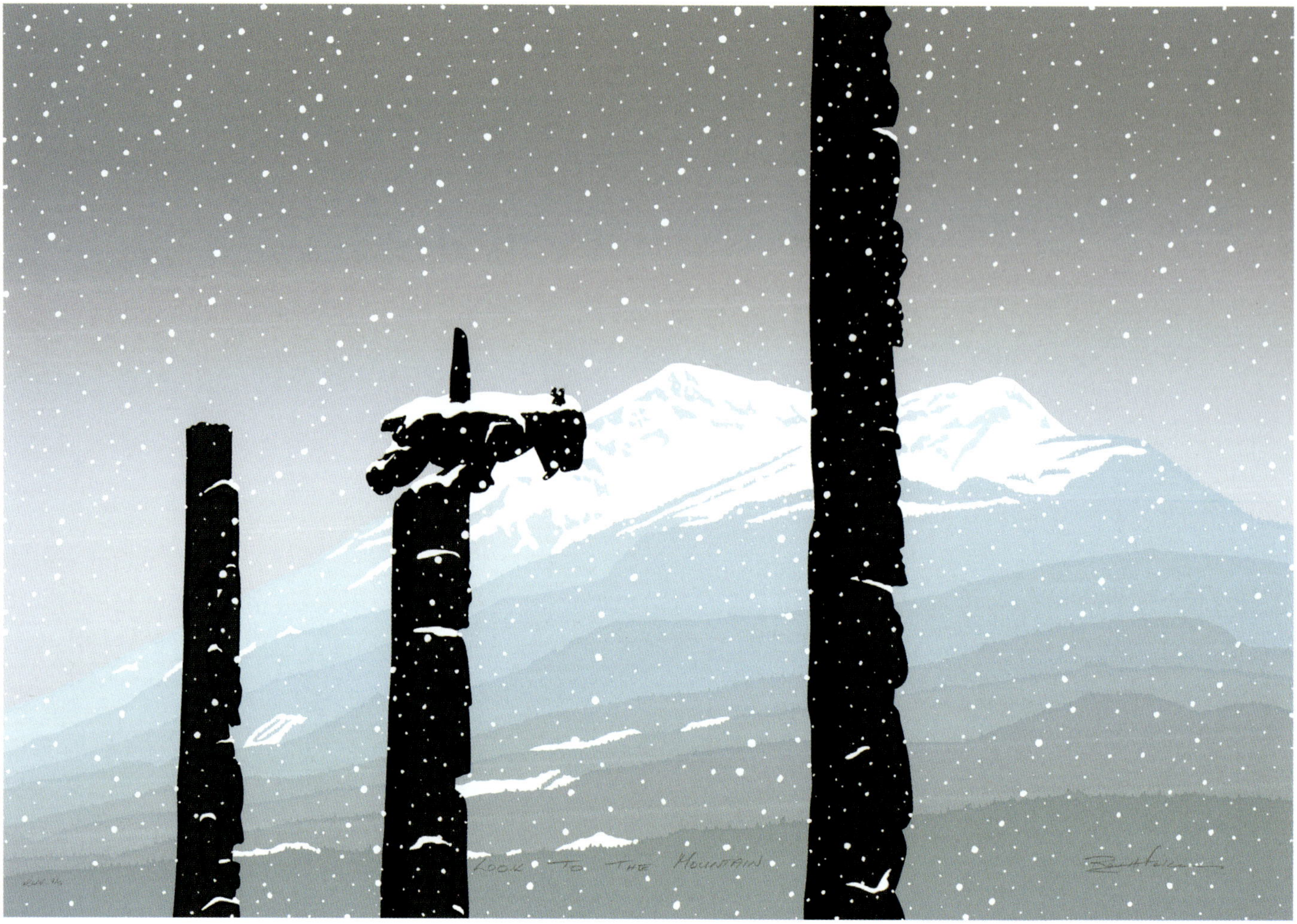

Look to the Mountain 1987

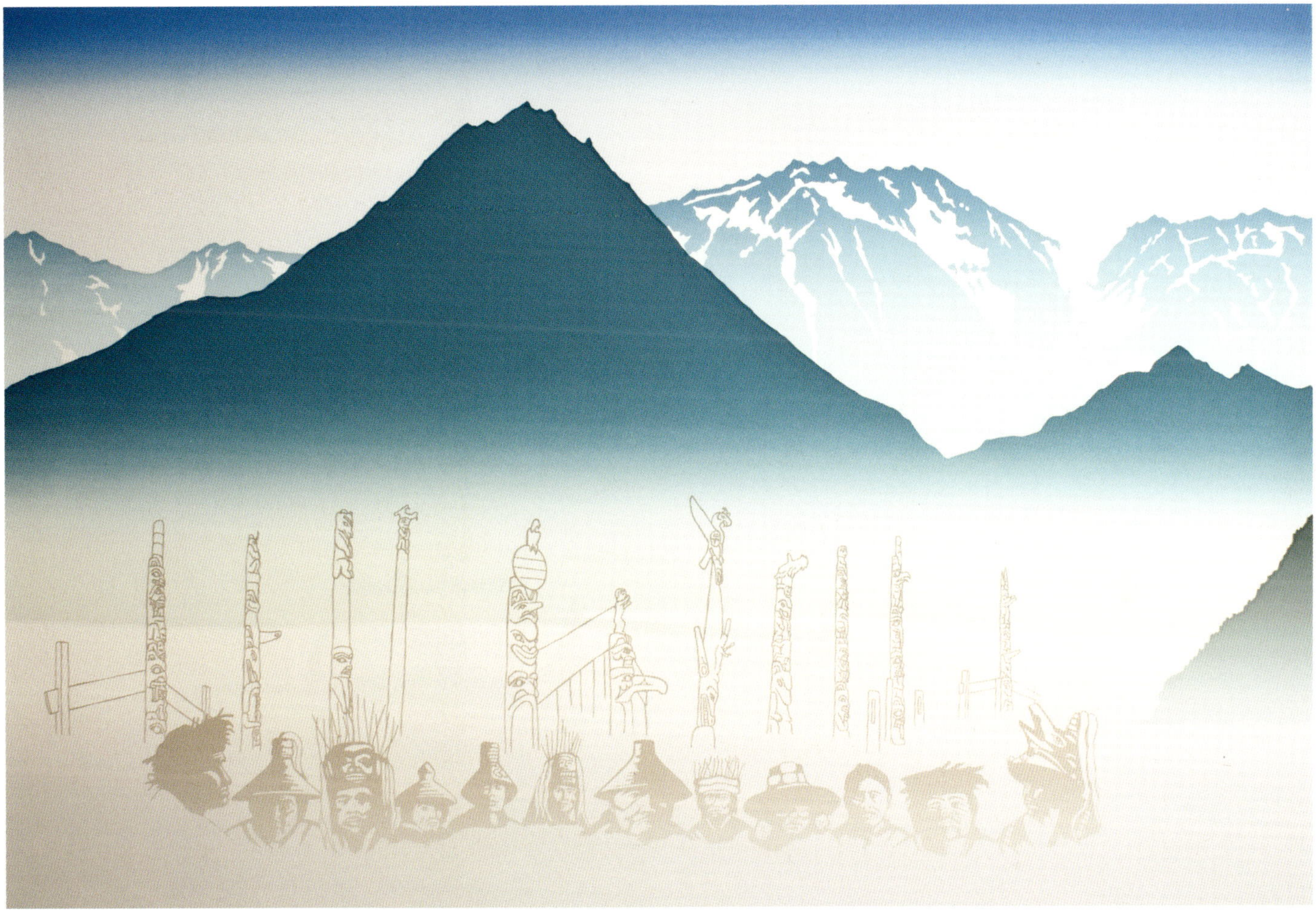

A Meeting of Chiefs 1987

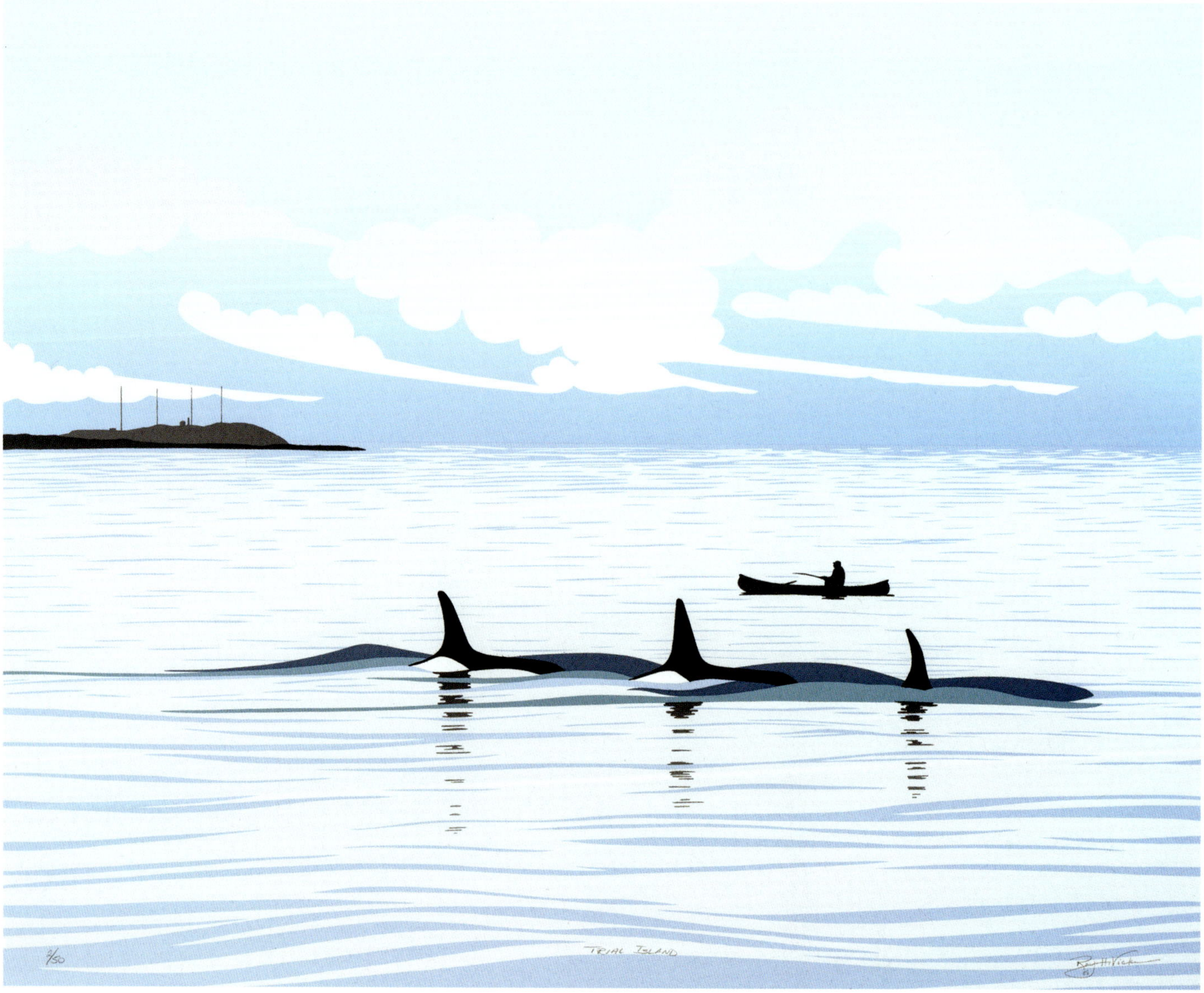

Victoria series: *Trial Island* 1988

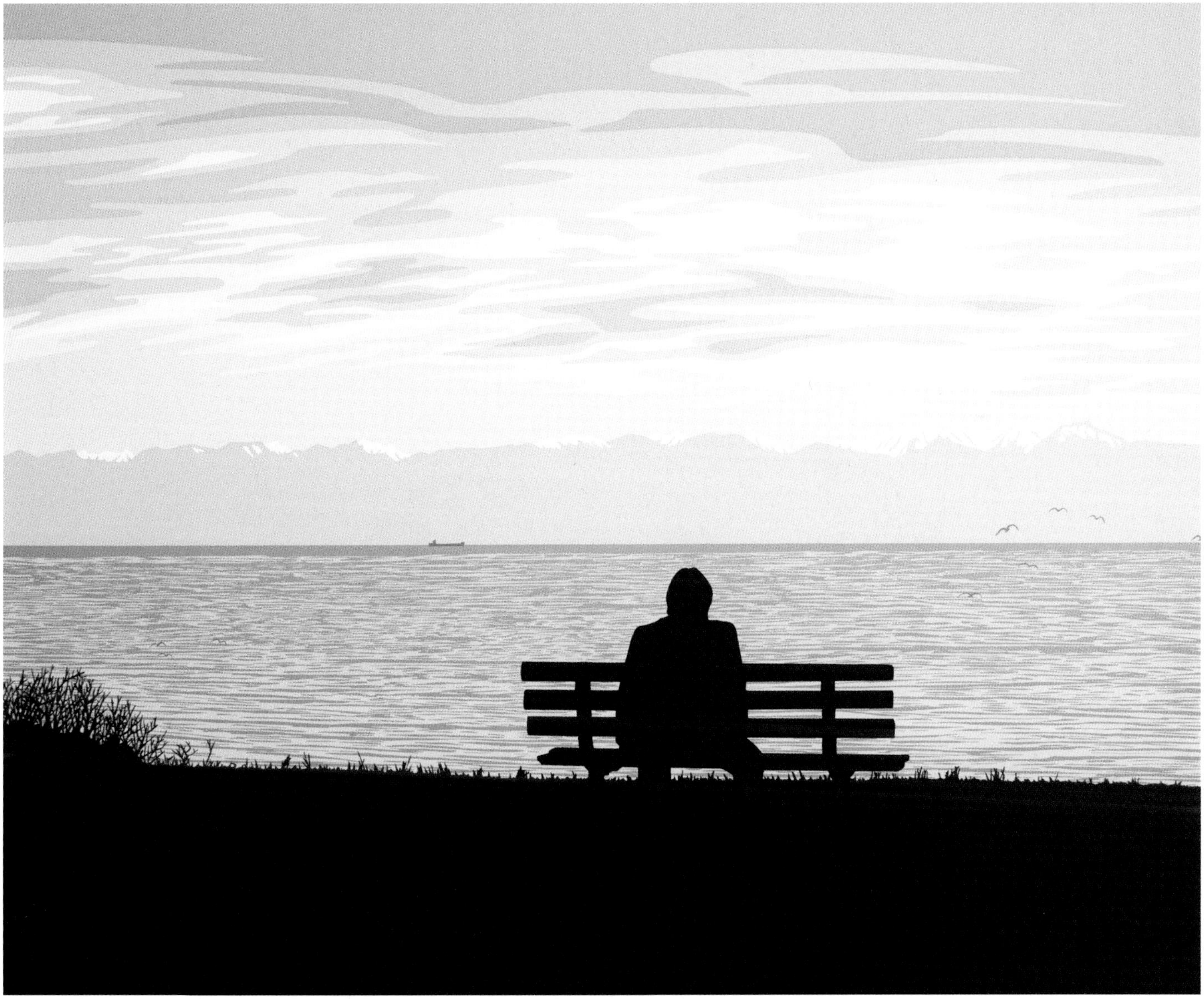

Victoria series: *Where Is Kitkatla?* 1988

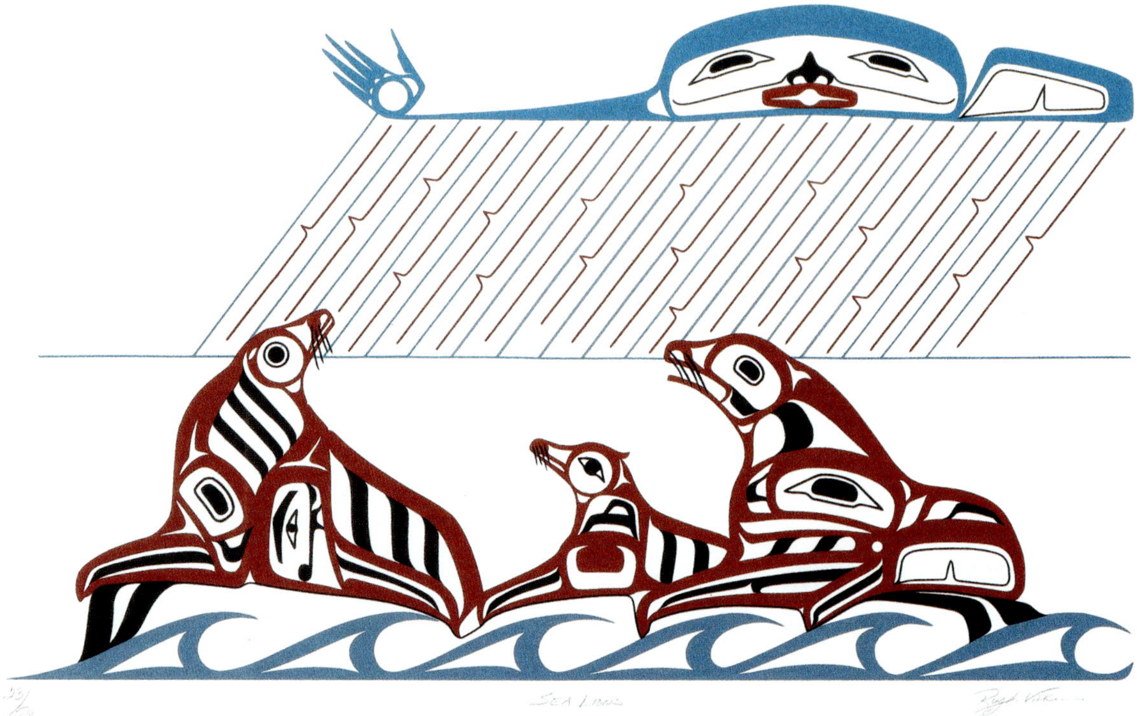

Sea Lions 1988

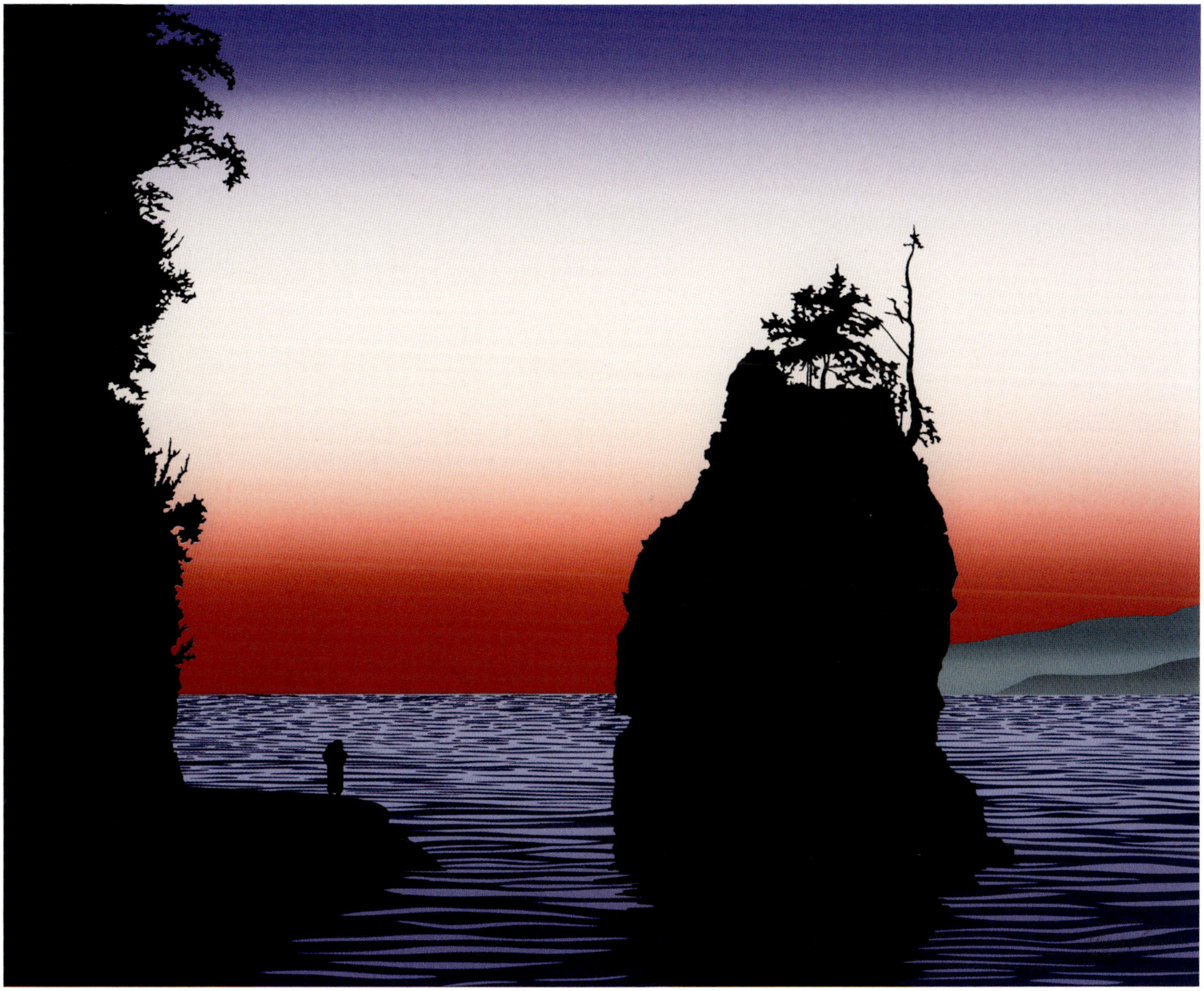

Vancouver series: *Siwash Rock* 1988

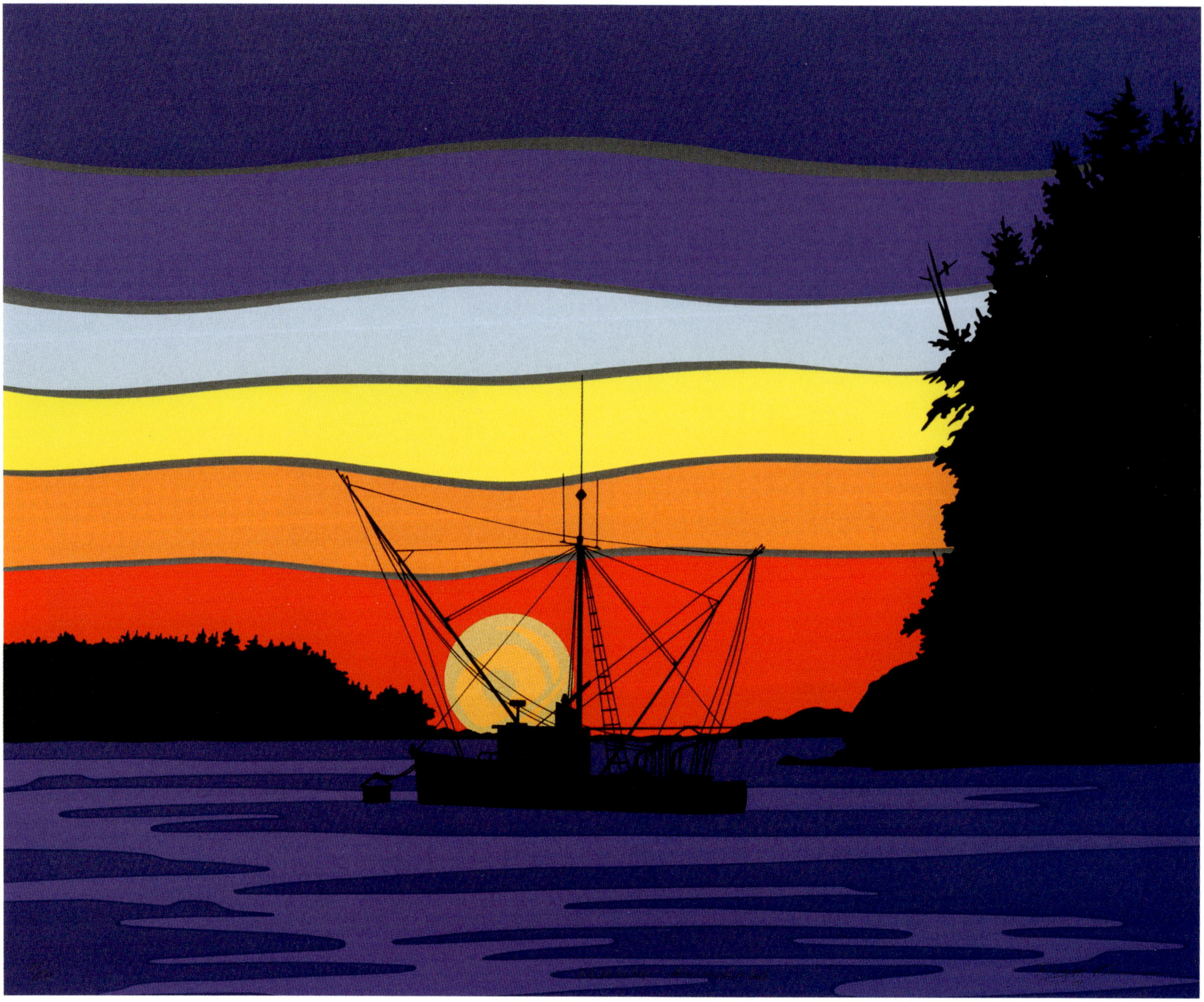

Evening Anchorage 1989

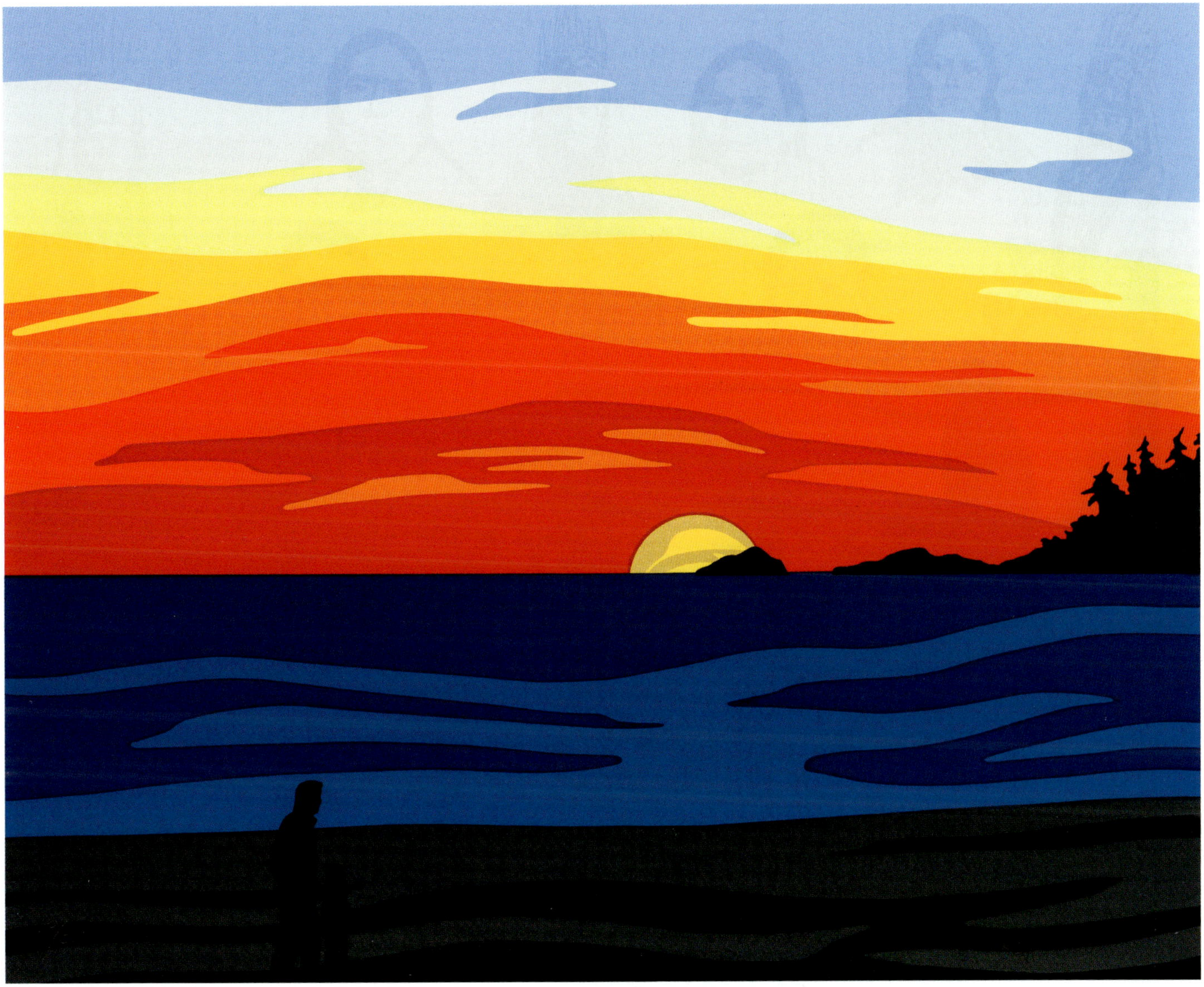

The Elders Are Watching 1990

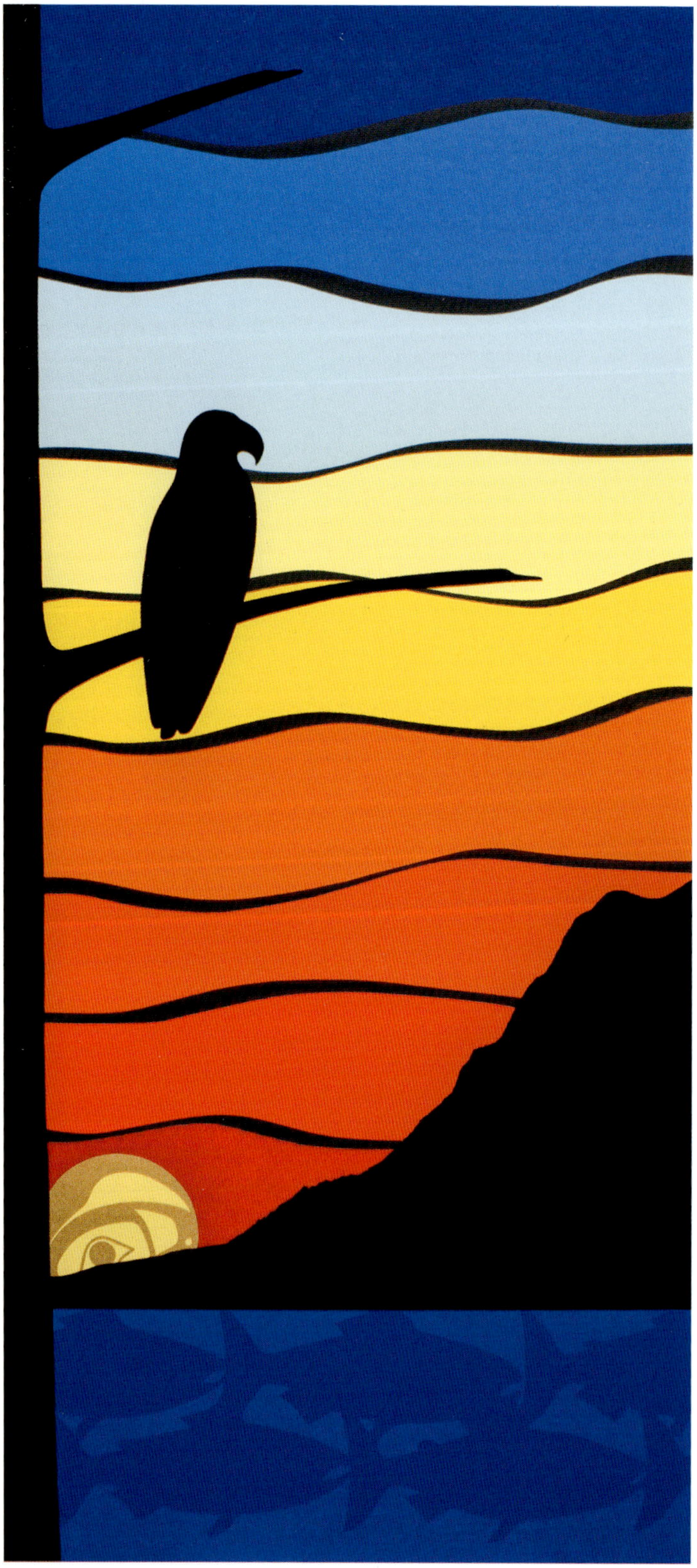

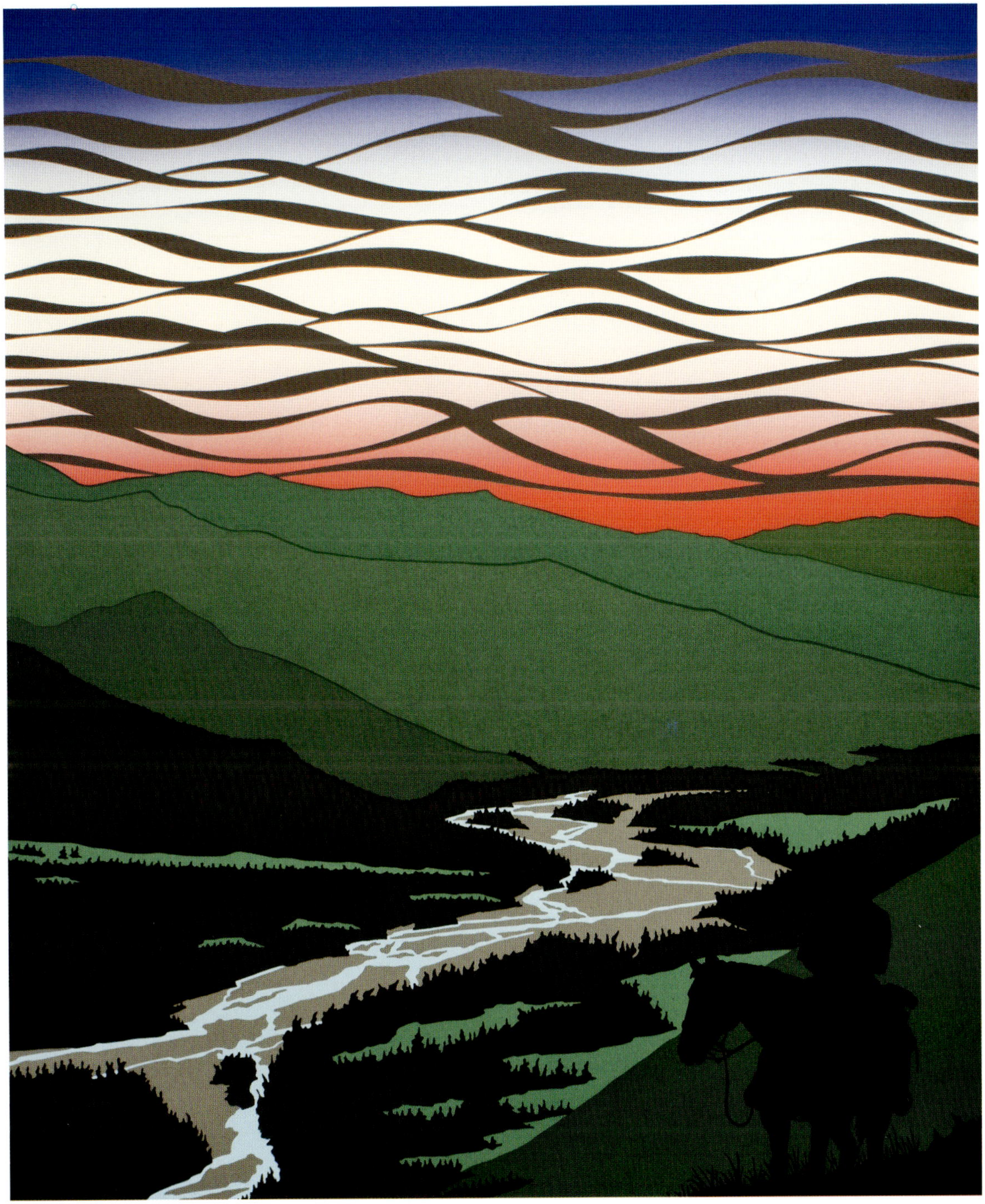

Eagle's Sunset 1991 | *September Smoke* 1991

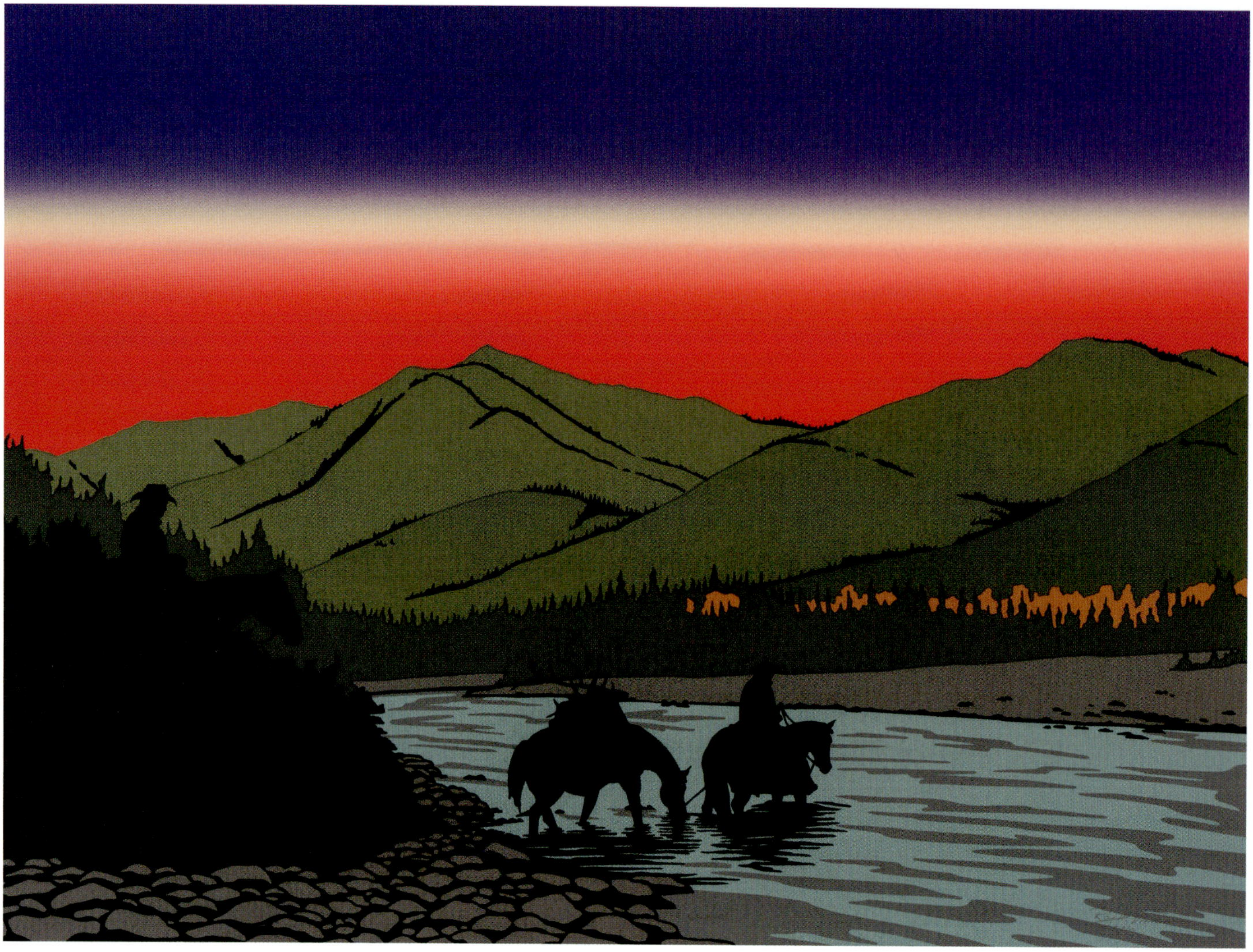

The Crossing 1991

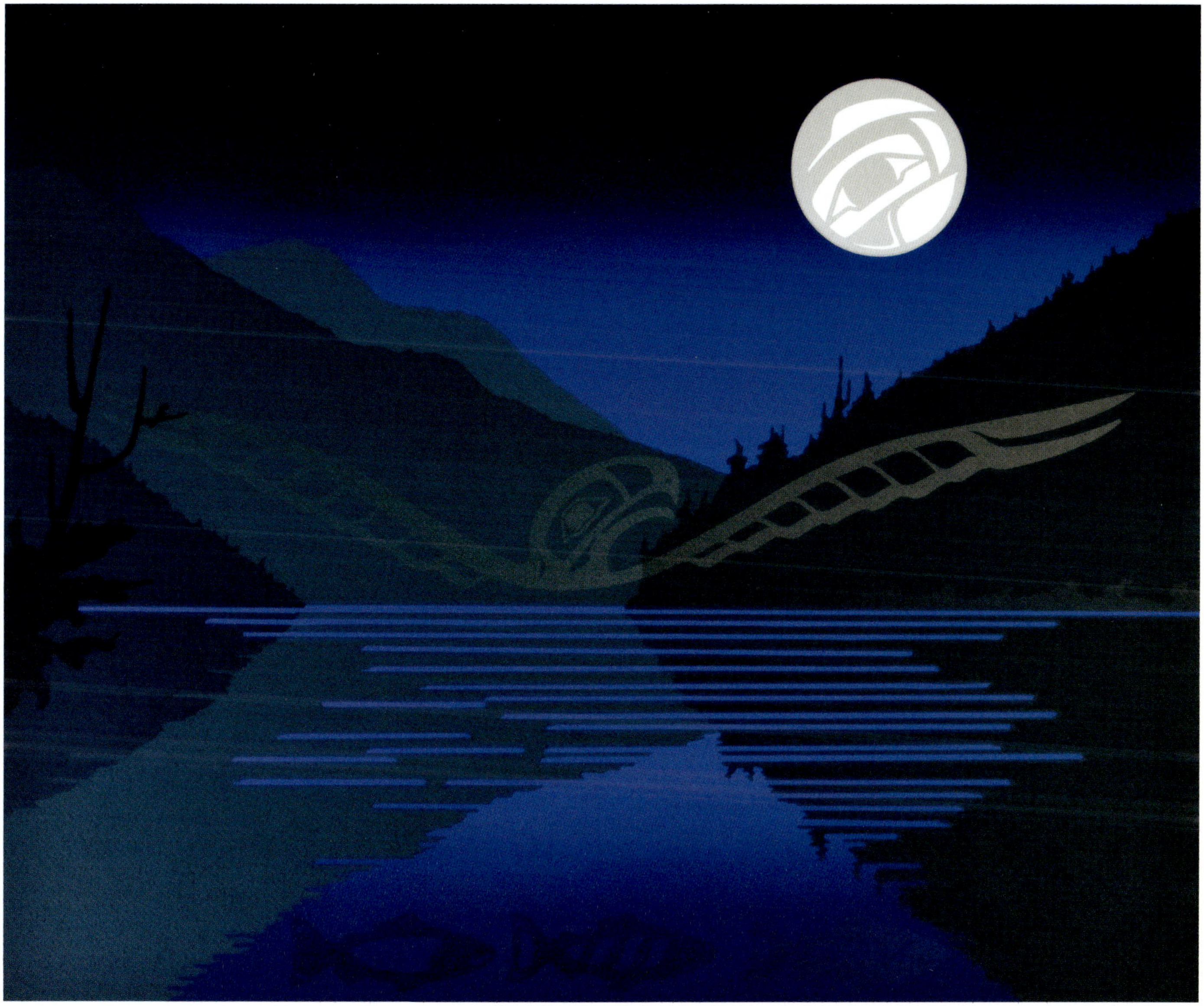

Tyee Moon 1992

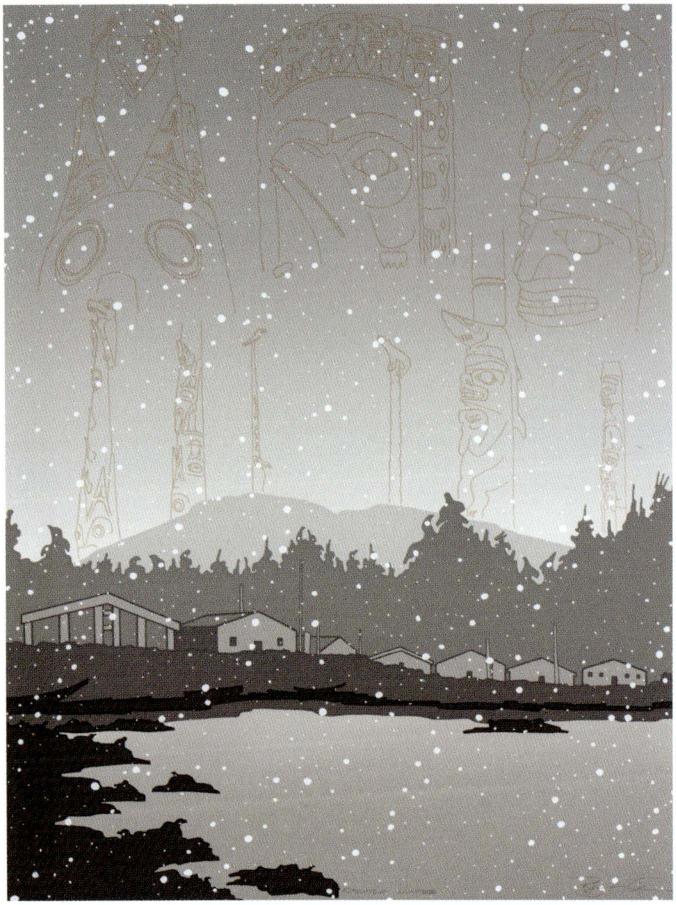

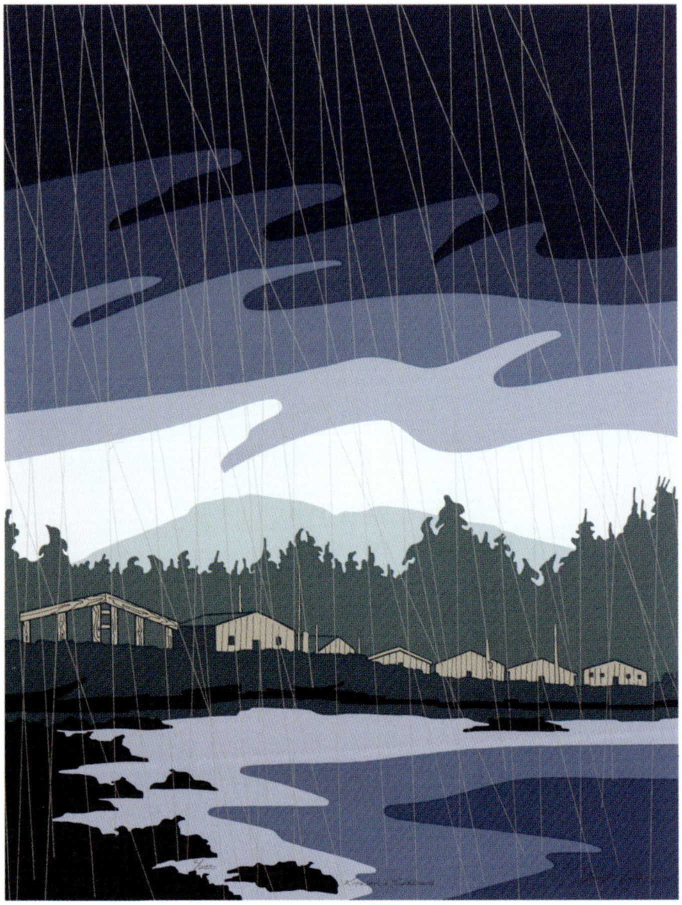

Kitkatla Winter 1993 | *Kitkatla Spring* 1993

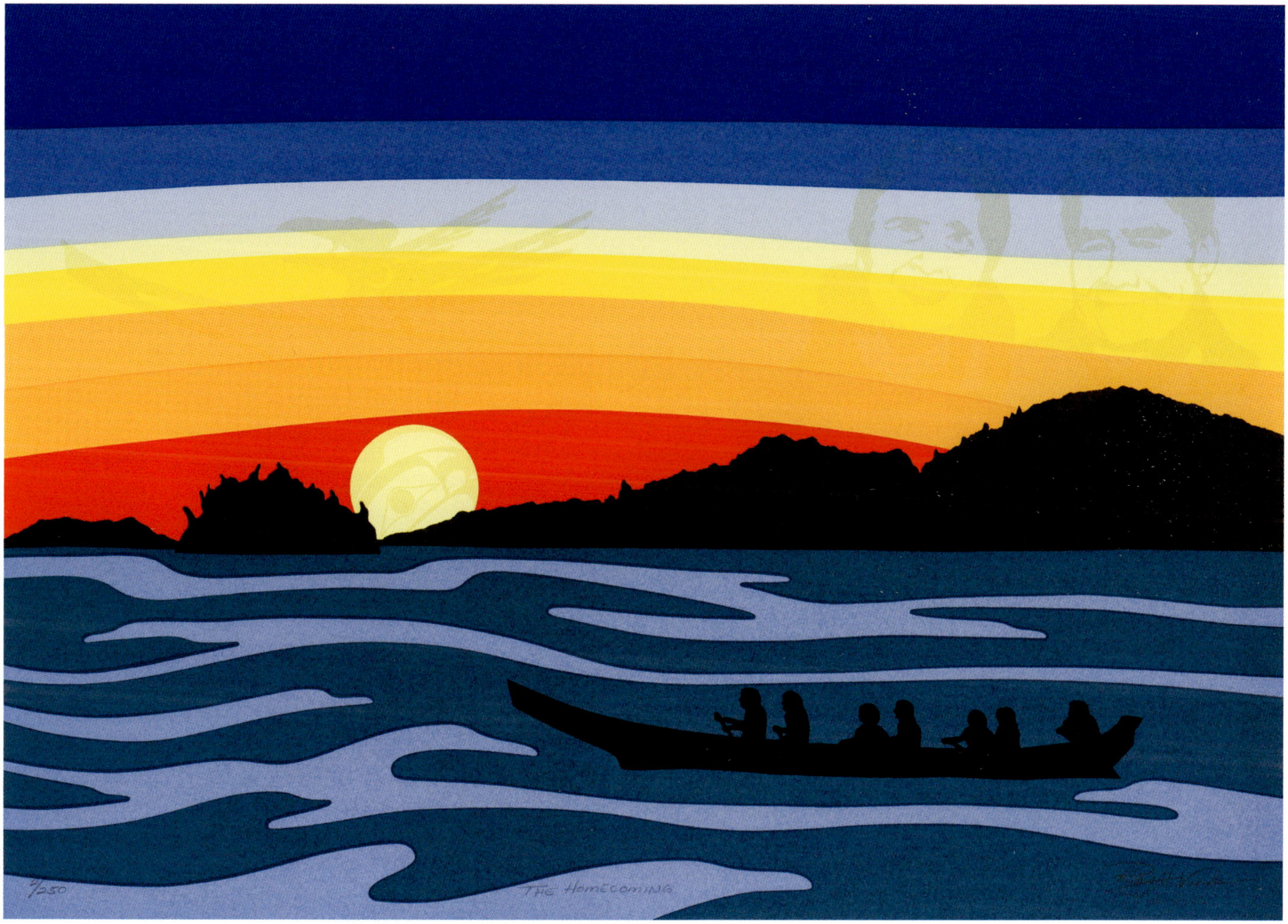

The Homecoming 1993

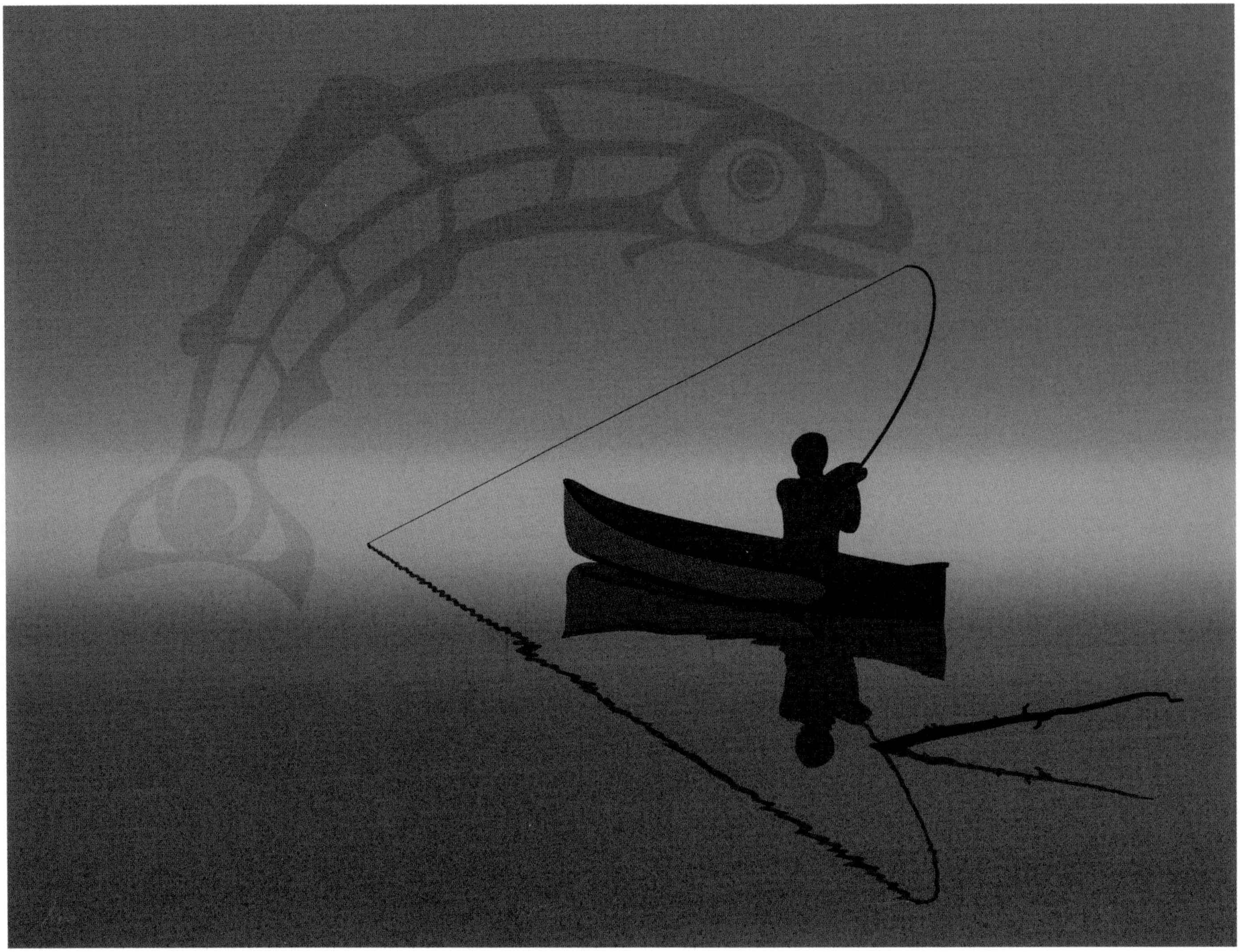

Megin Mist 1993

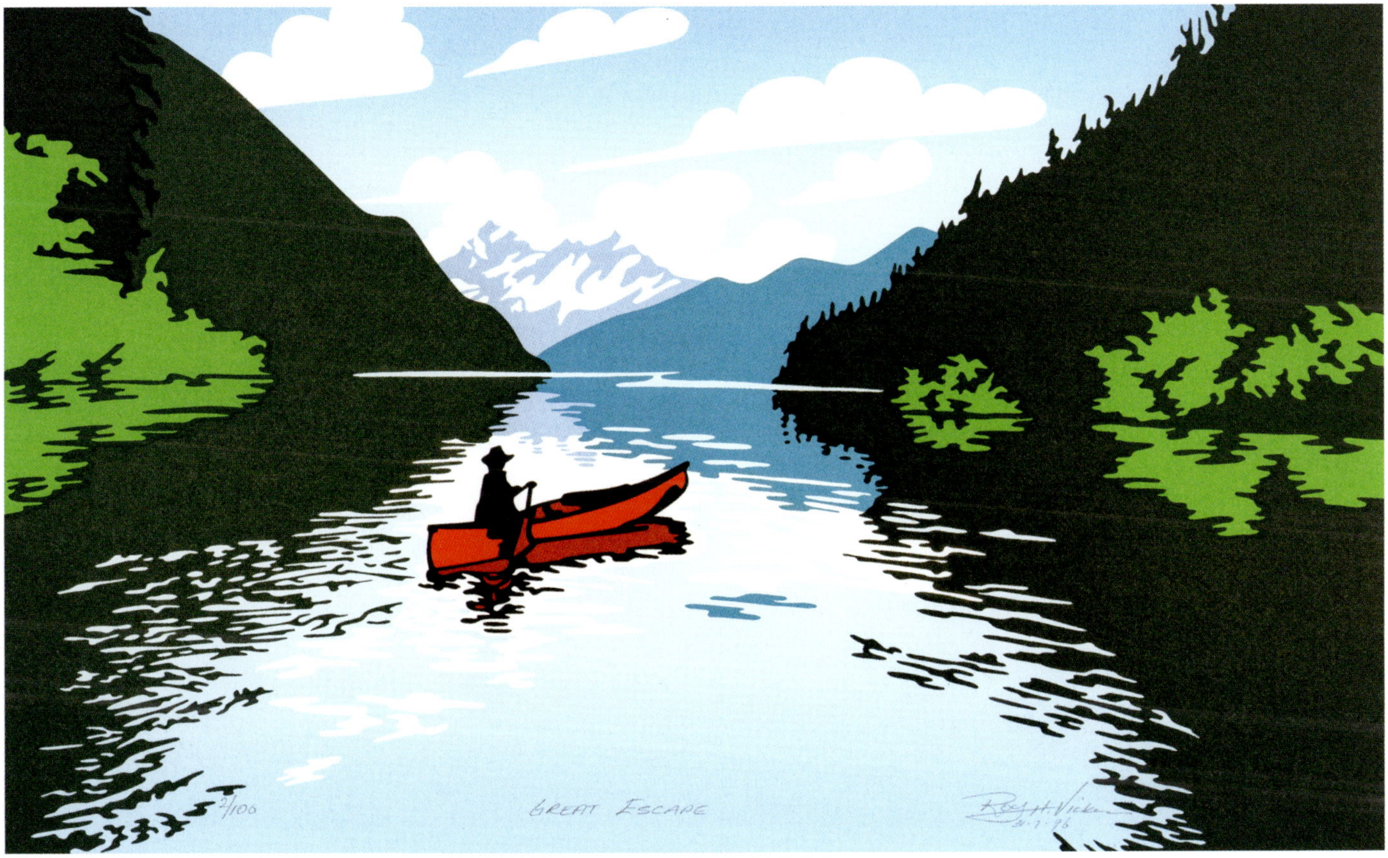

Great Escape 1996

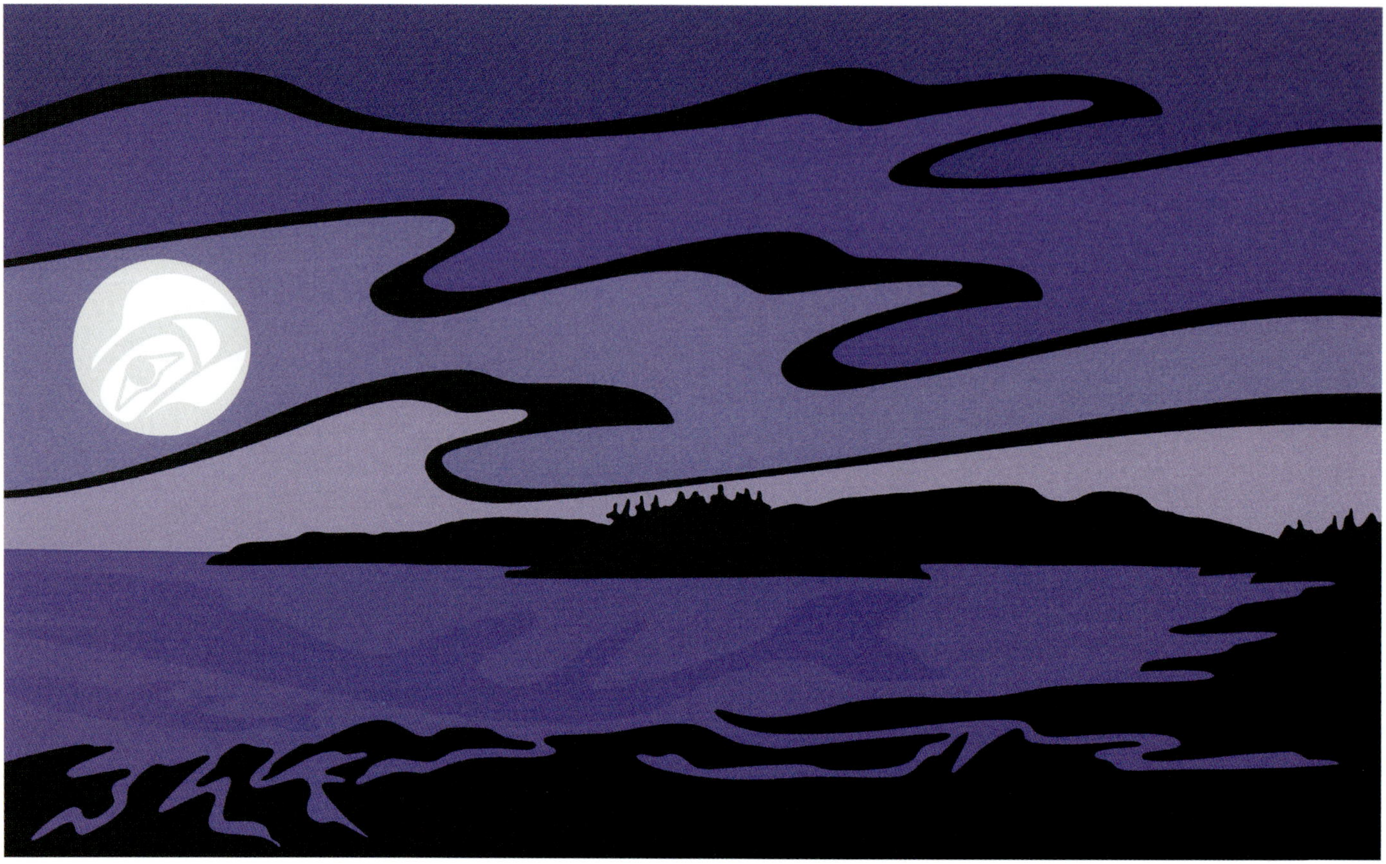

Skidegate 1997

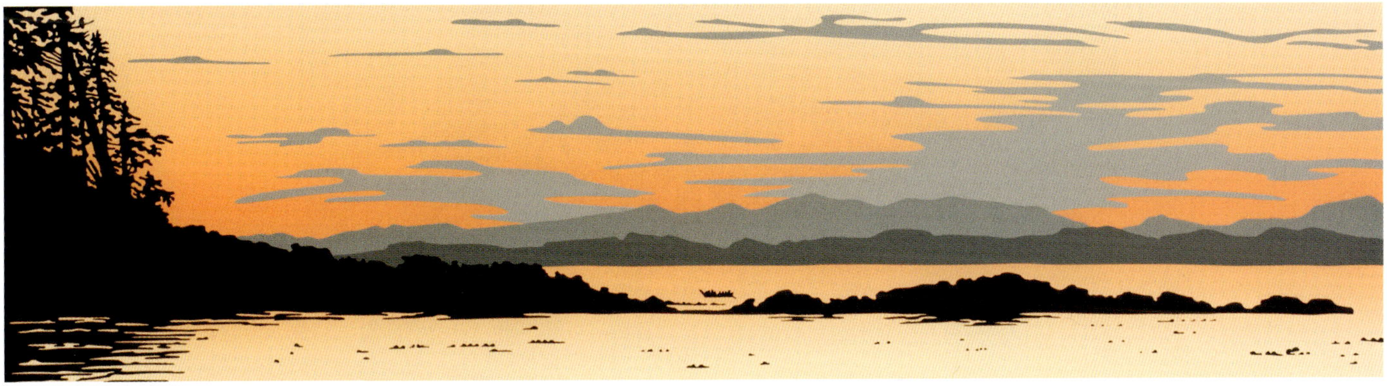

Nunsulsailus 1997

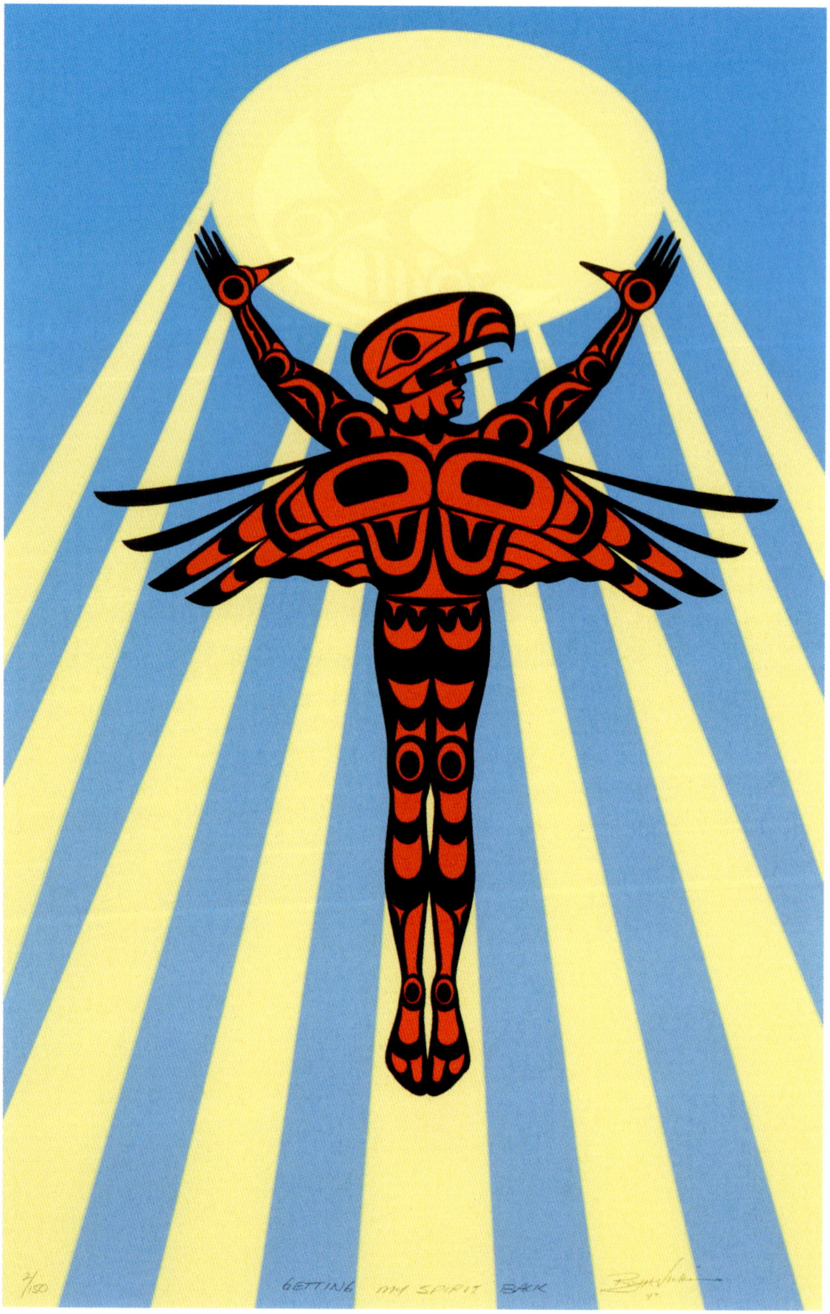

Getting My Spirit Back 1997

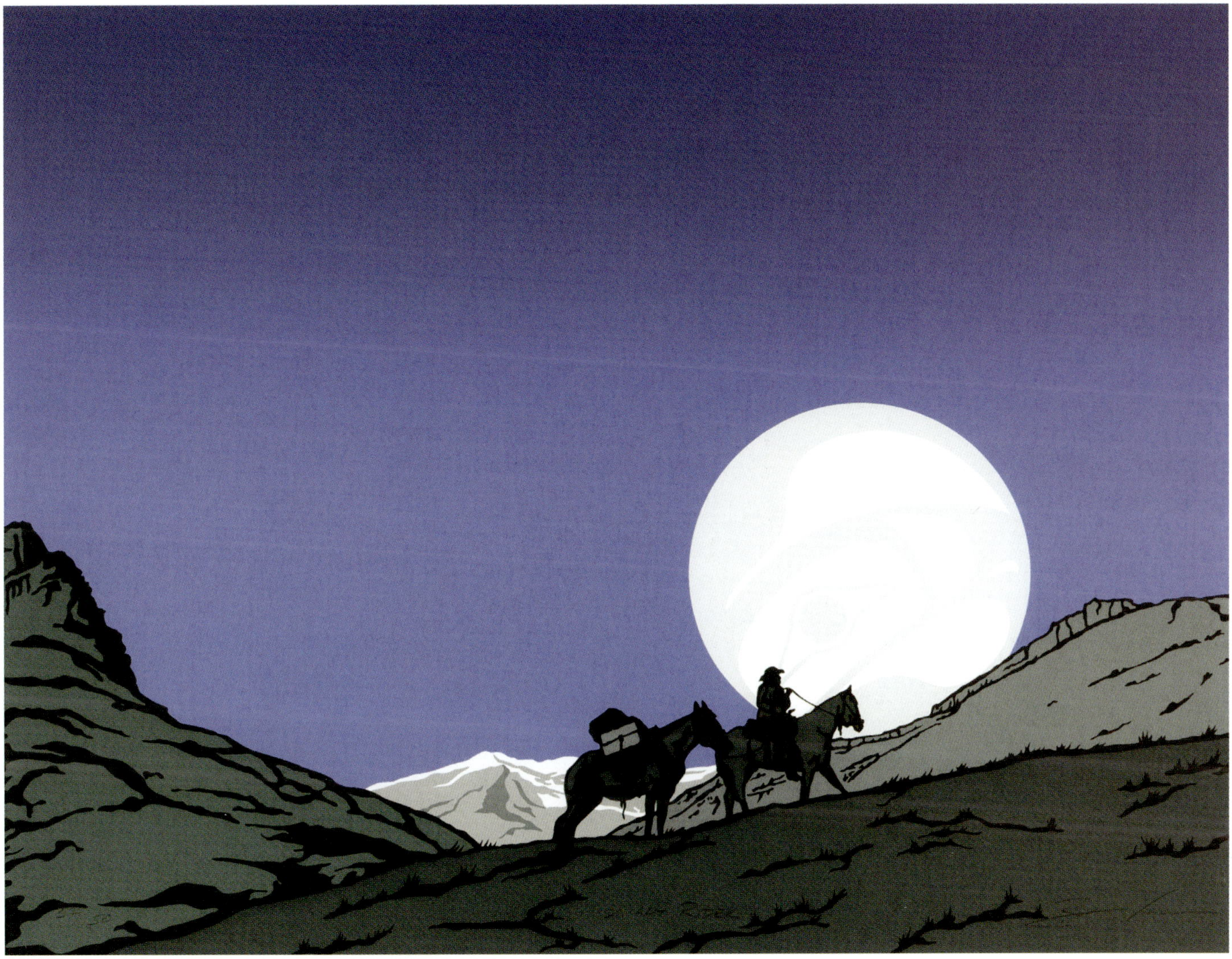

Midnight Rider 1998

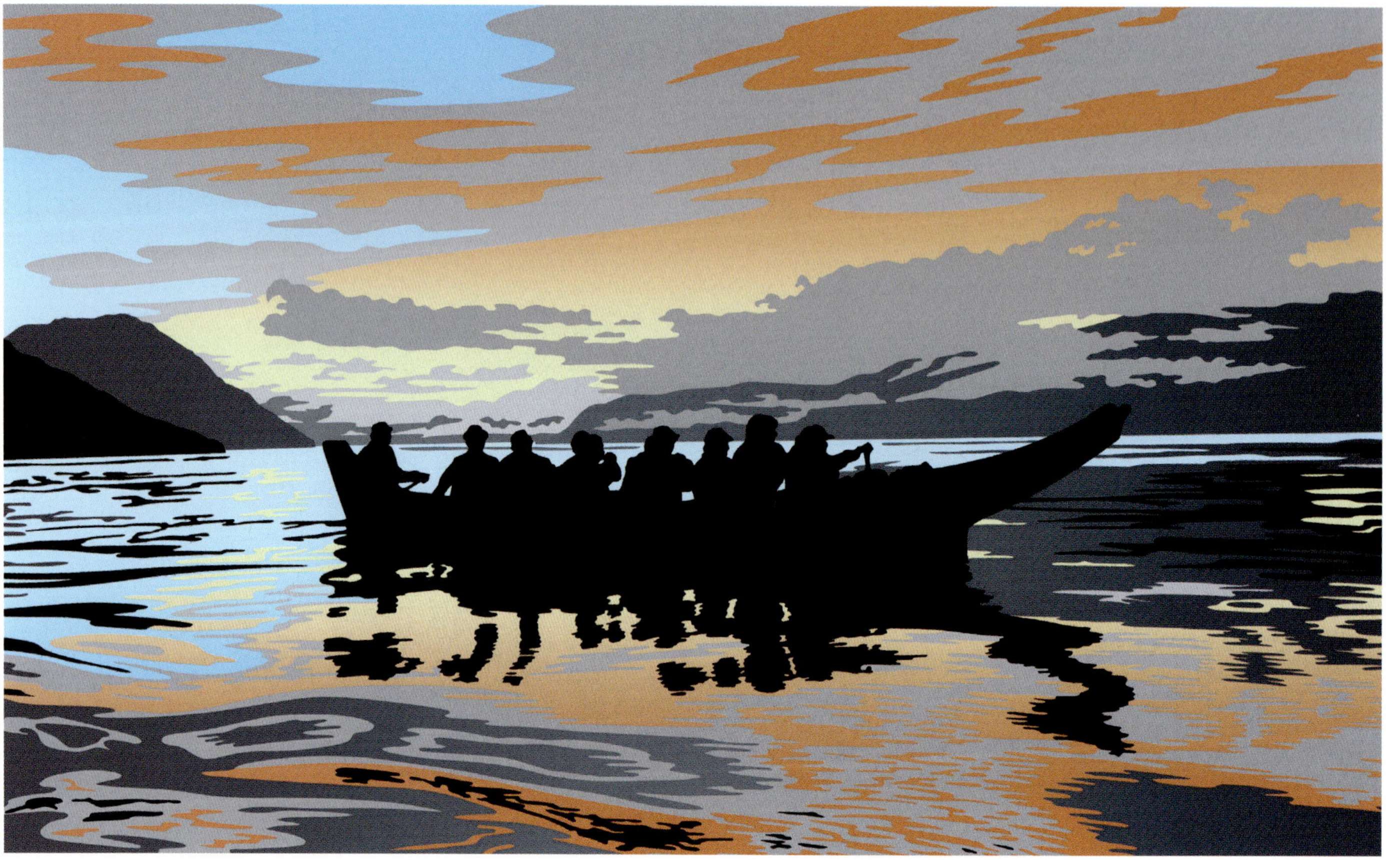

Kitasoo Dawn 1998

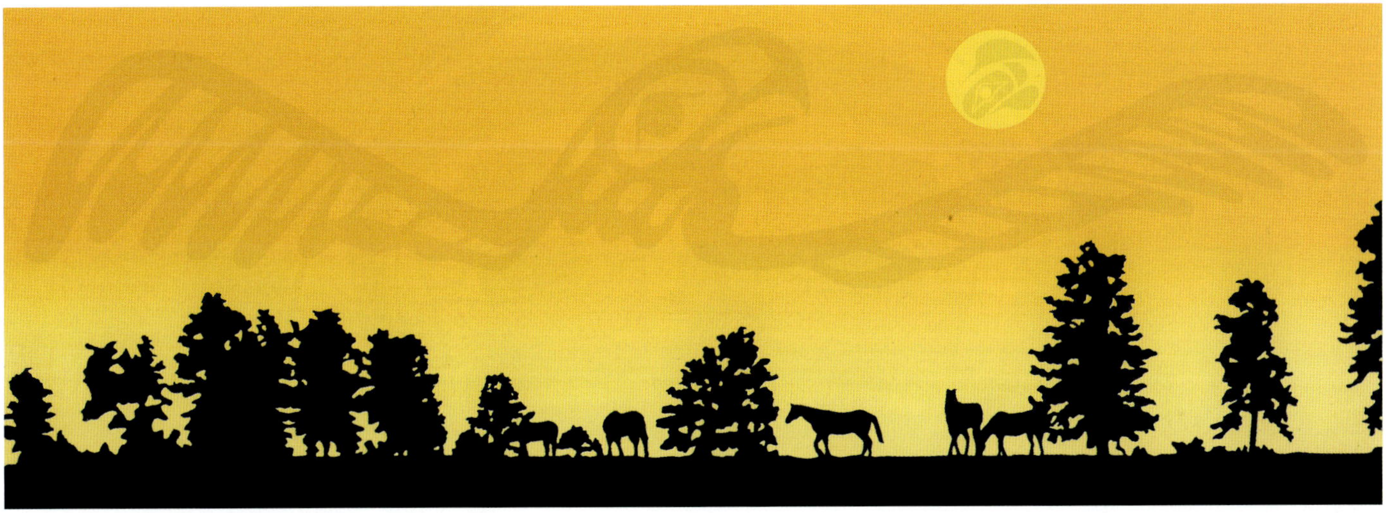

Koocanusa Sunrise 1999

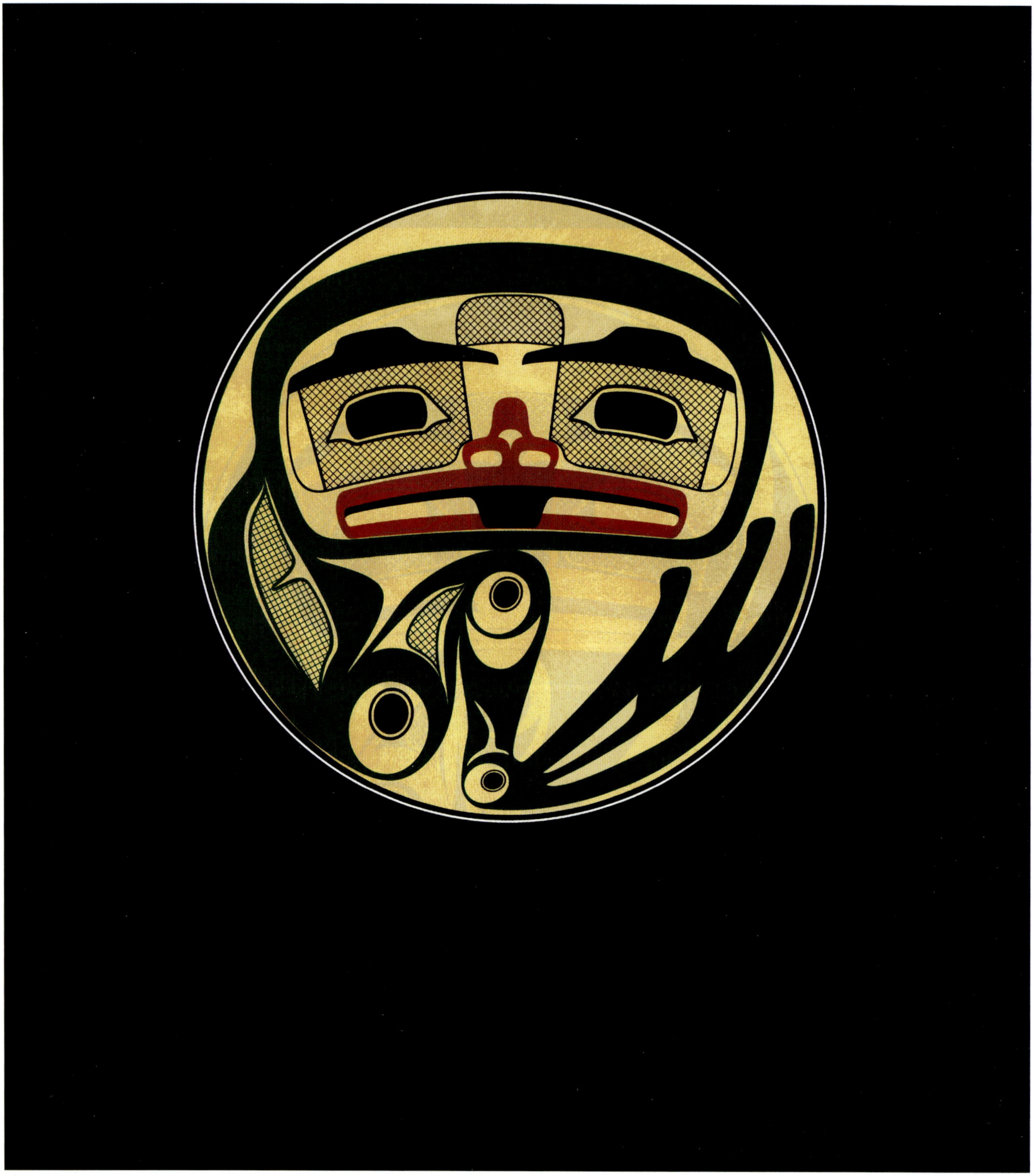

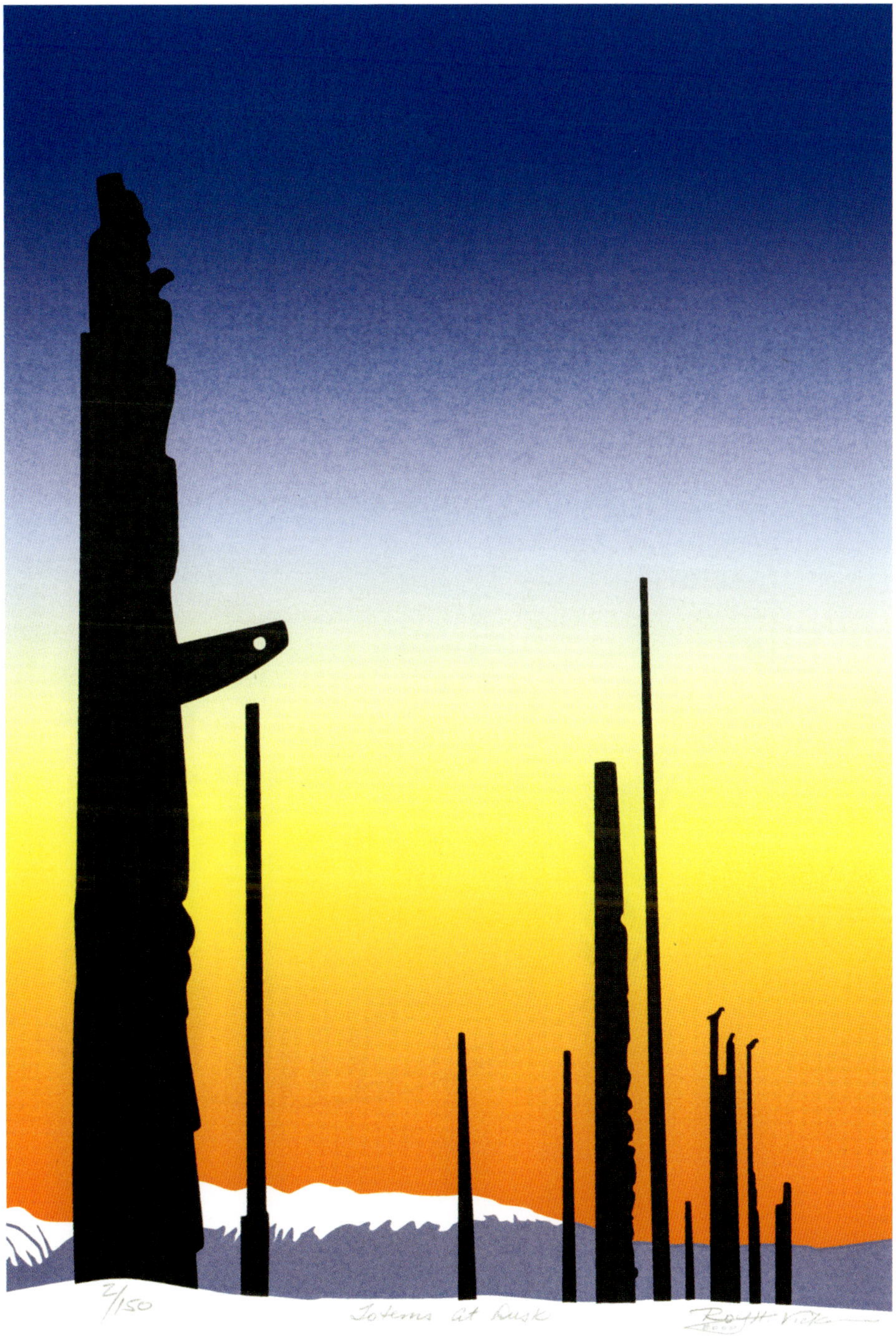

Frog Drum 2000 | *Totems at Dusk* 2000

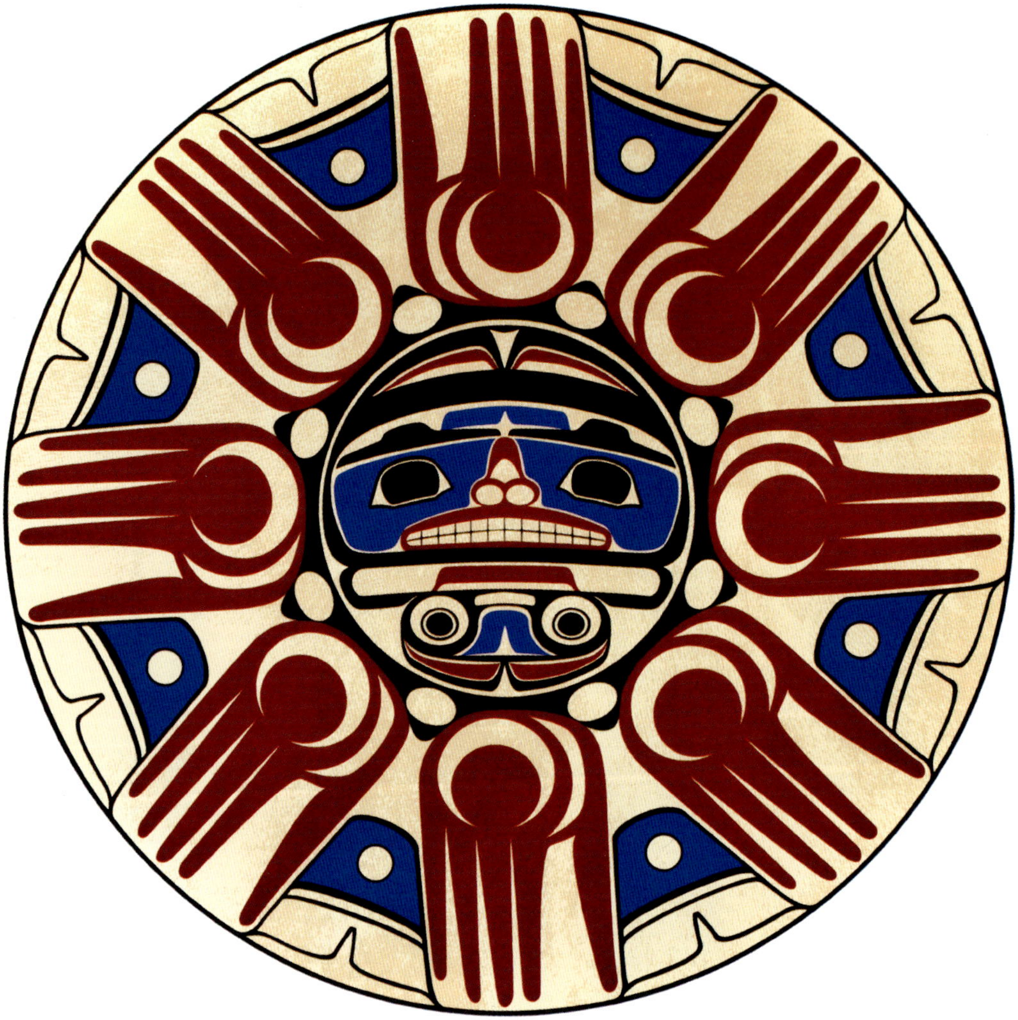

Opening Hands 2000 | *King Pacific Sunset* 2002

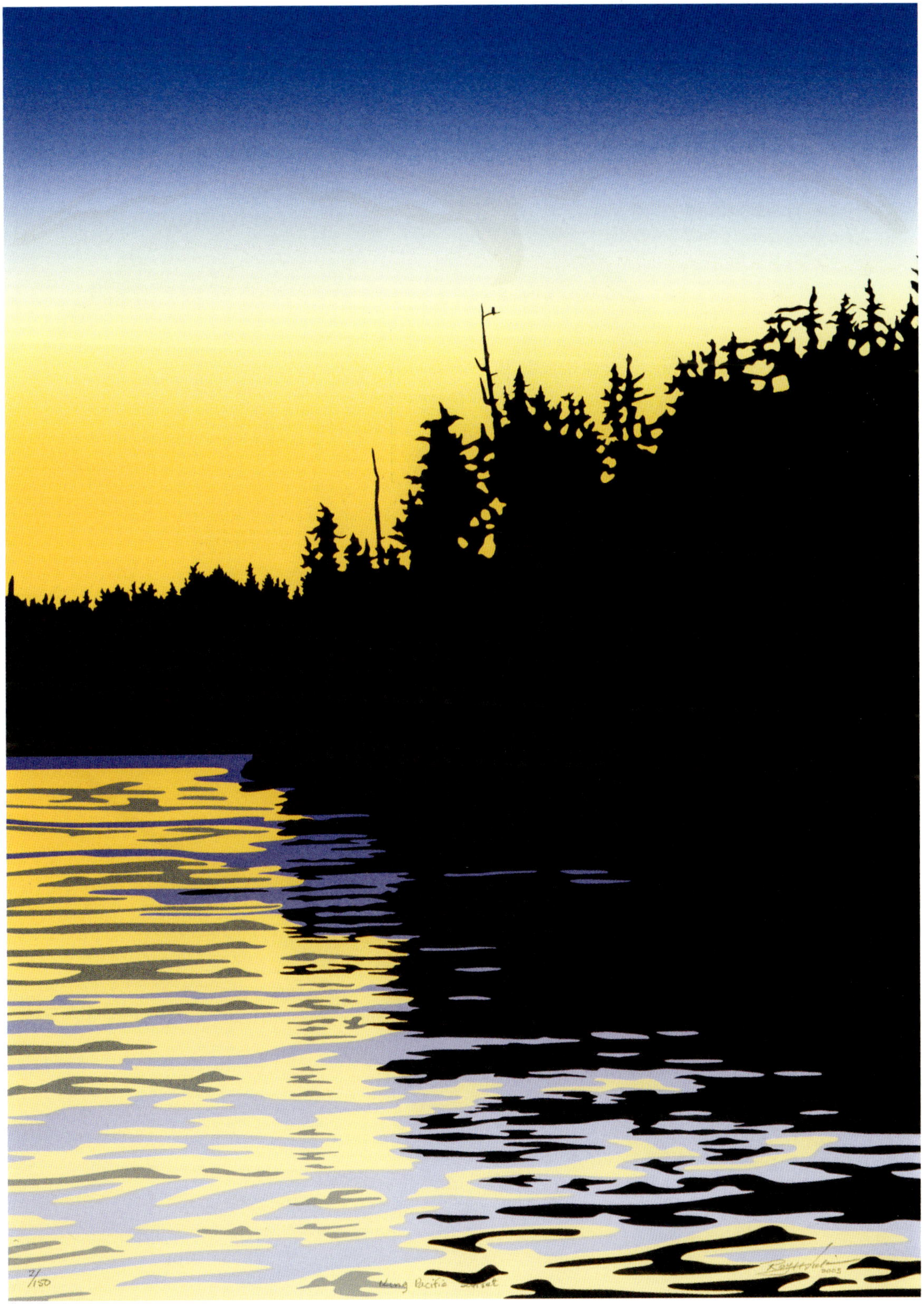
2/150
2005

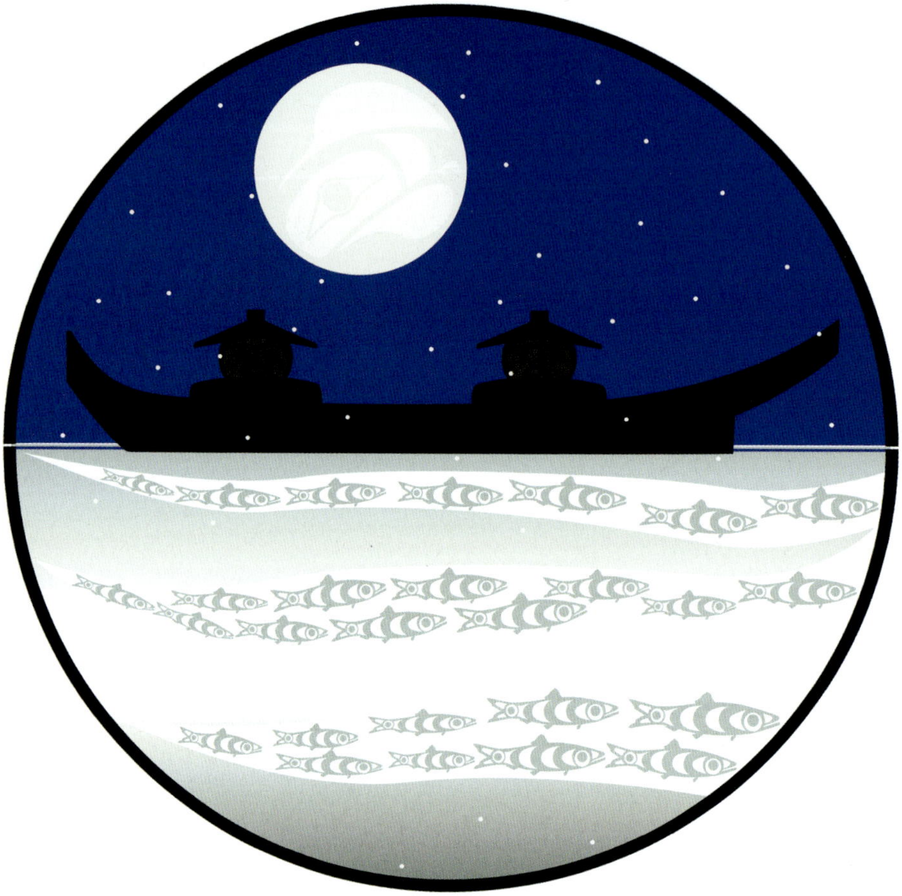

Milky Waters 2003

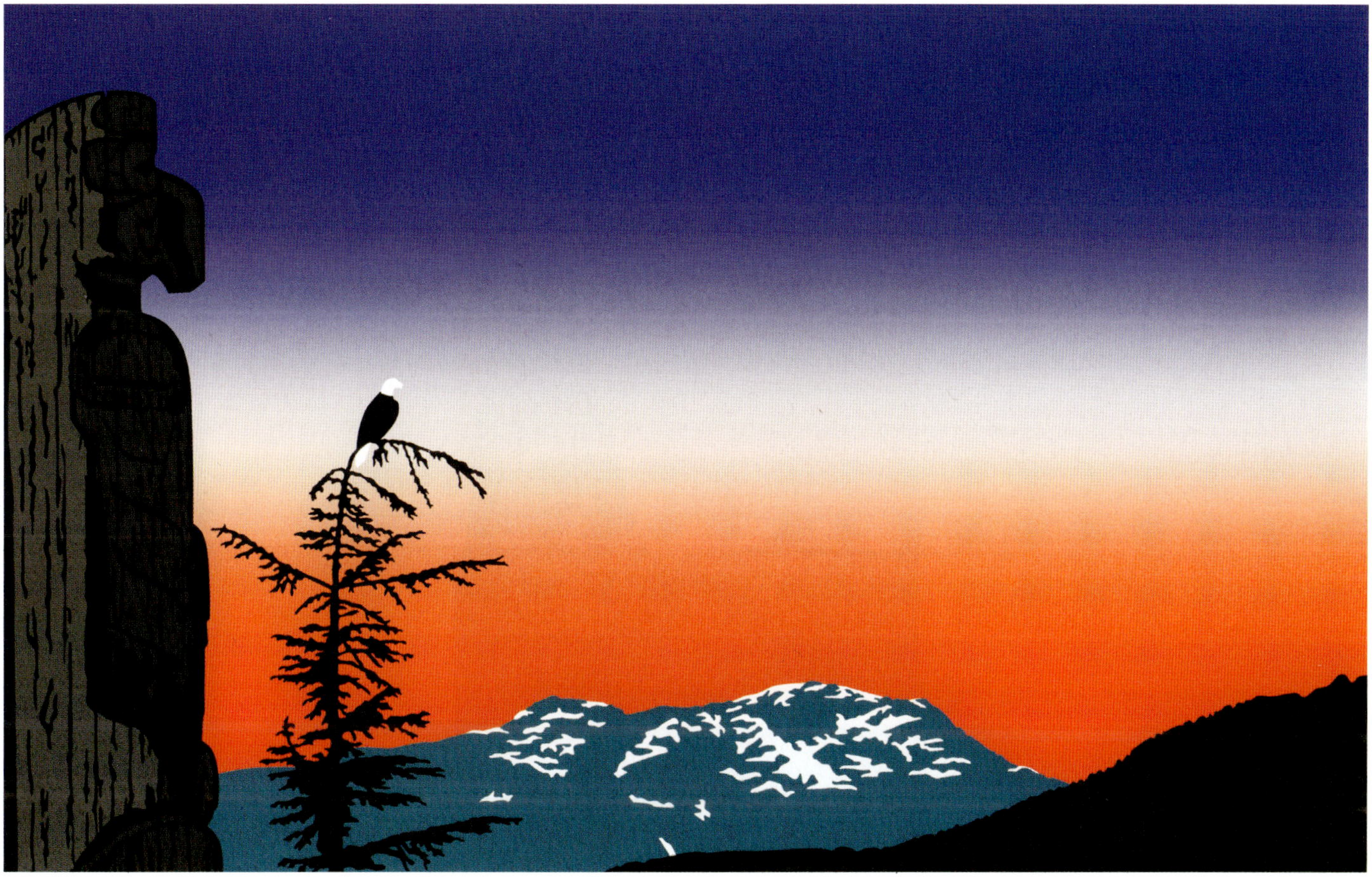

Eagle Totem 2003

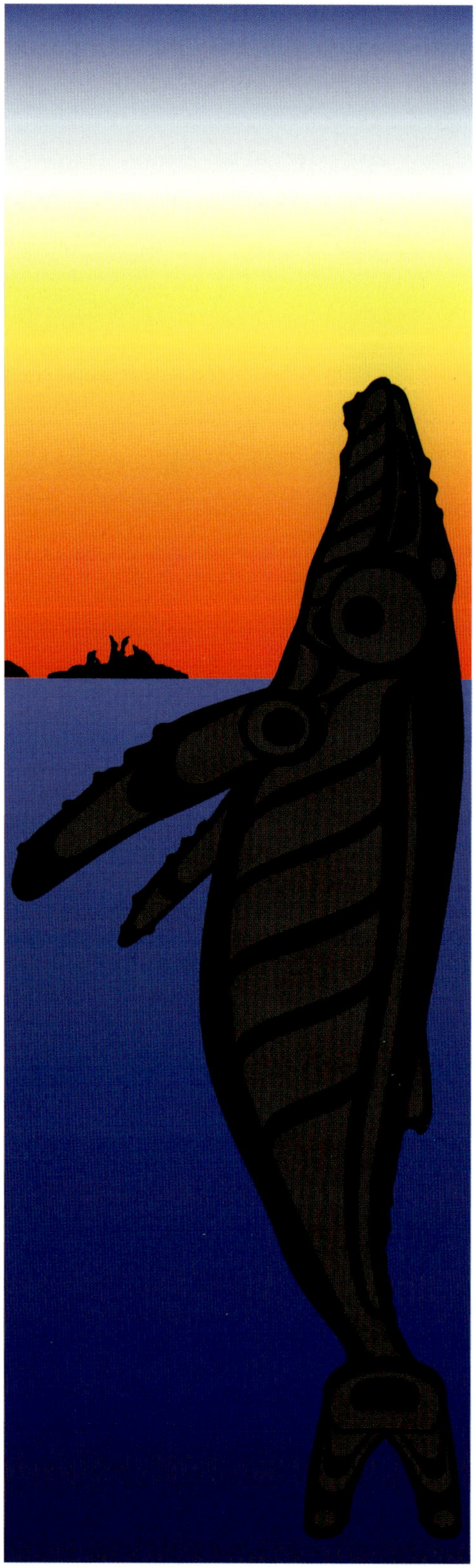

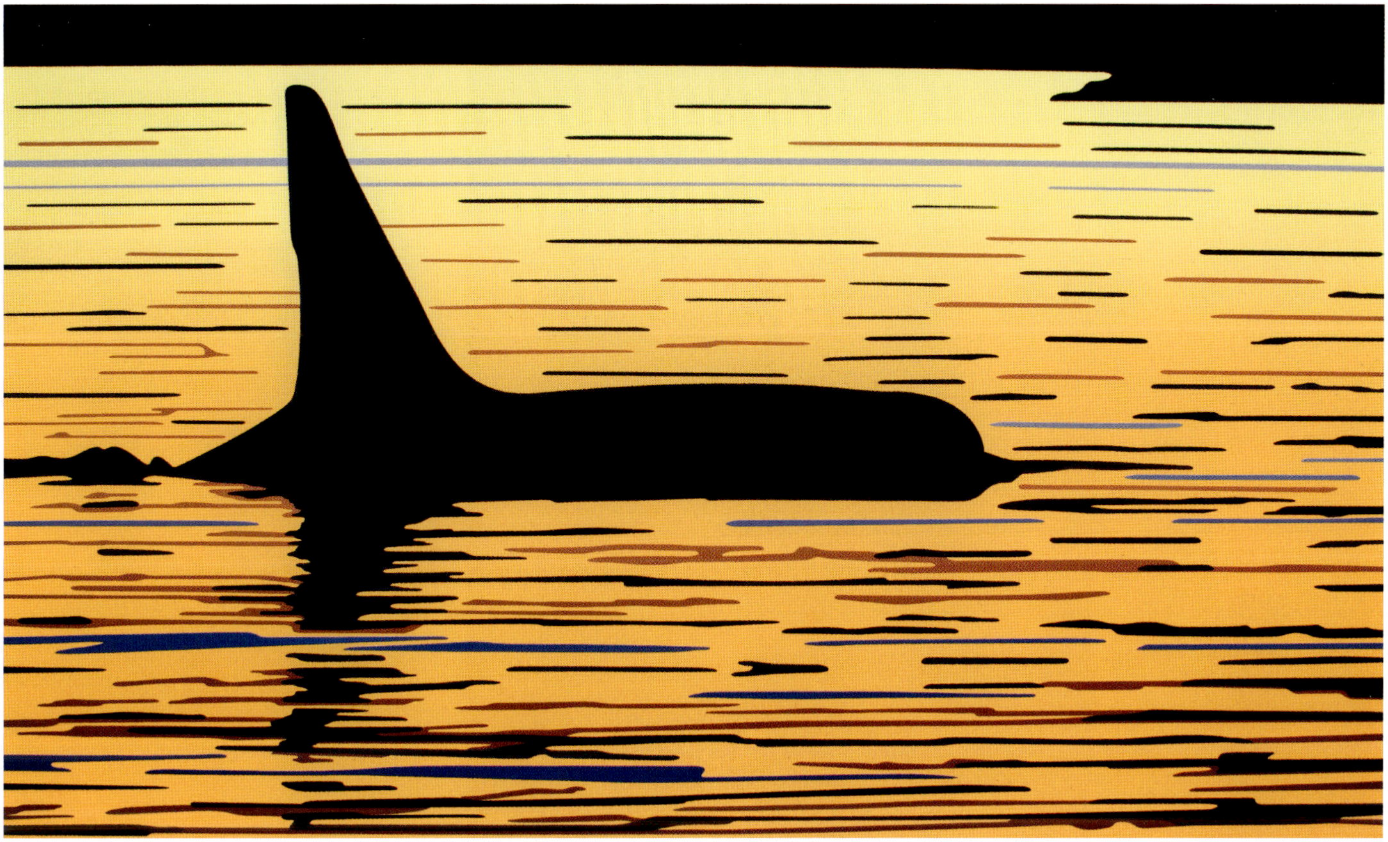

Spyhopping 2005 | *Orca Sunset* 2005

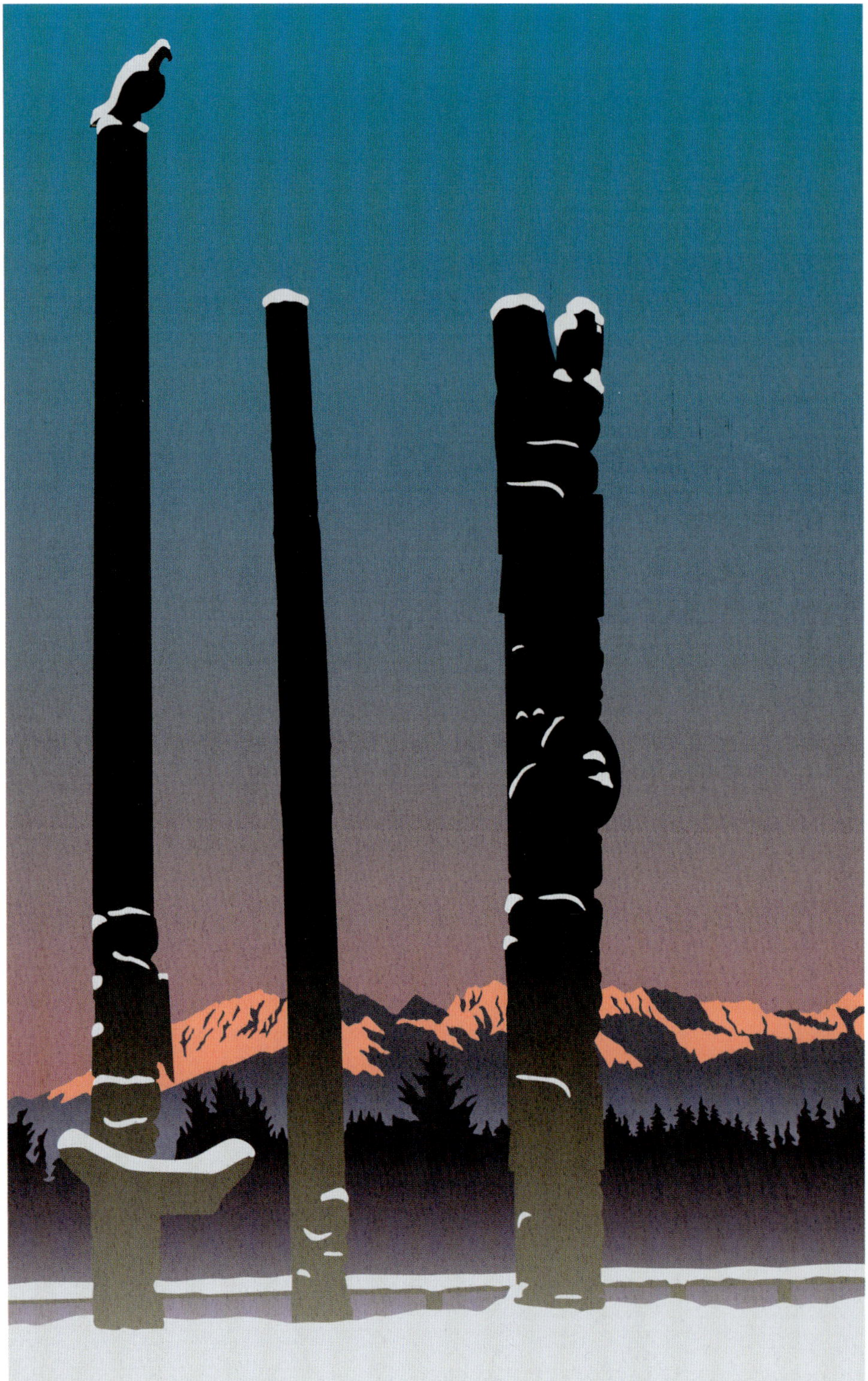
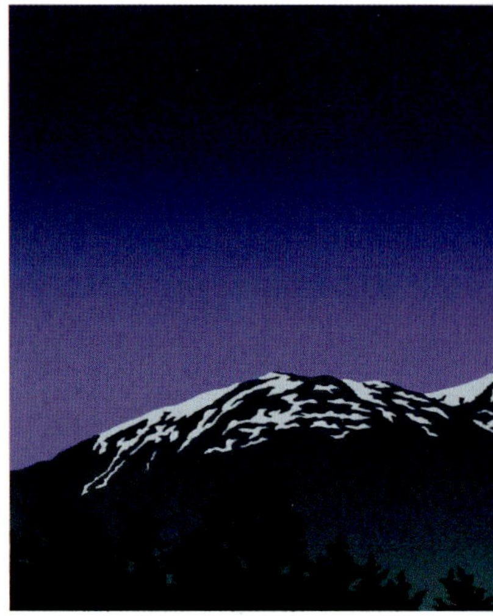

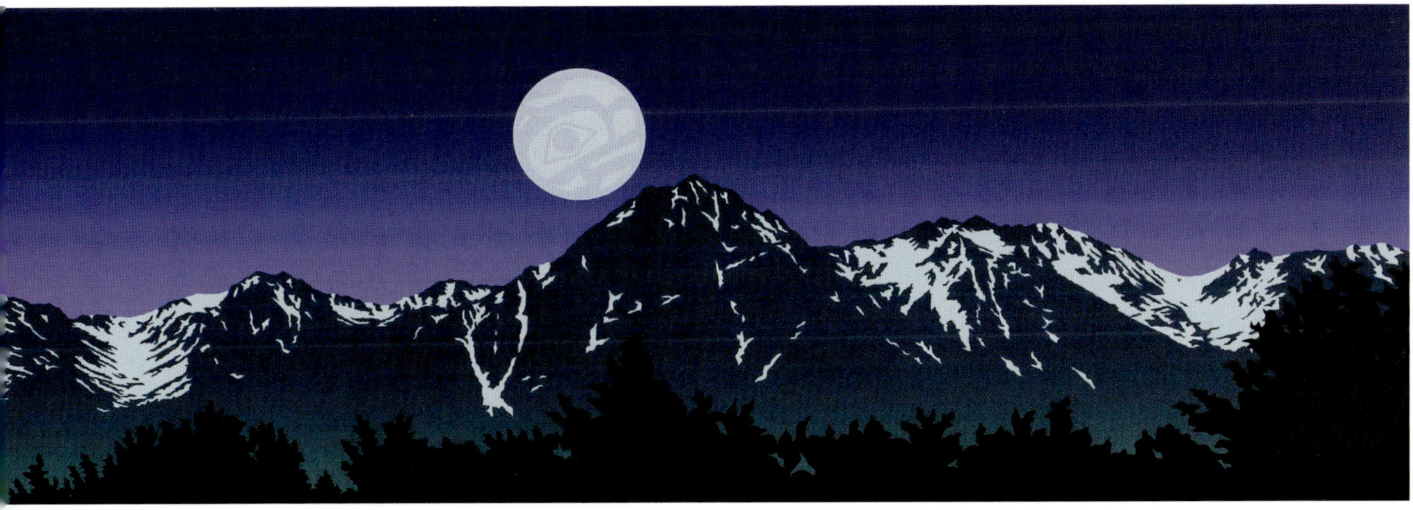

Totems in the Mist 2005 | *Bear Moon* 2006

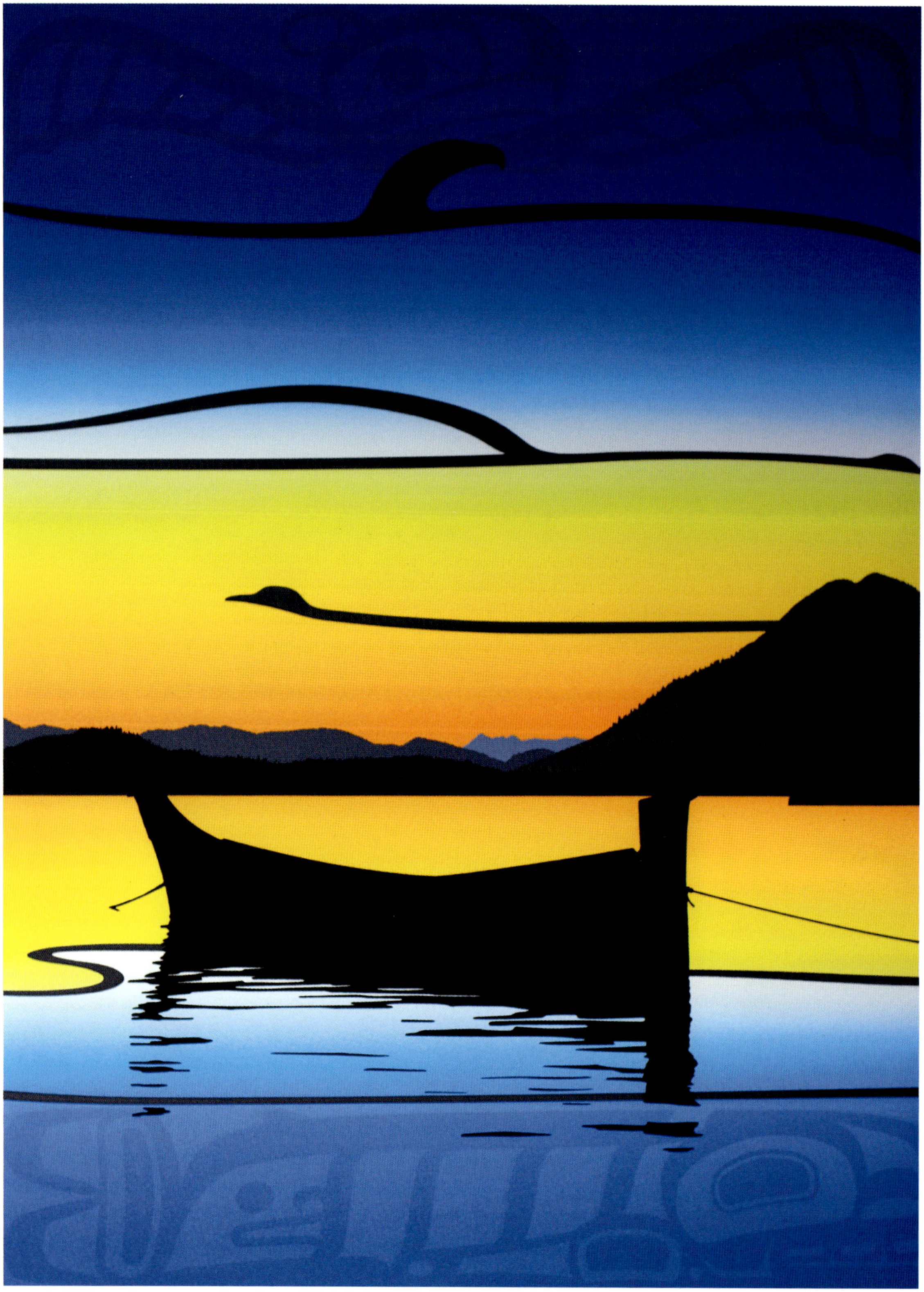

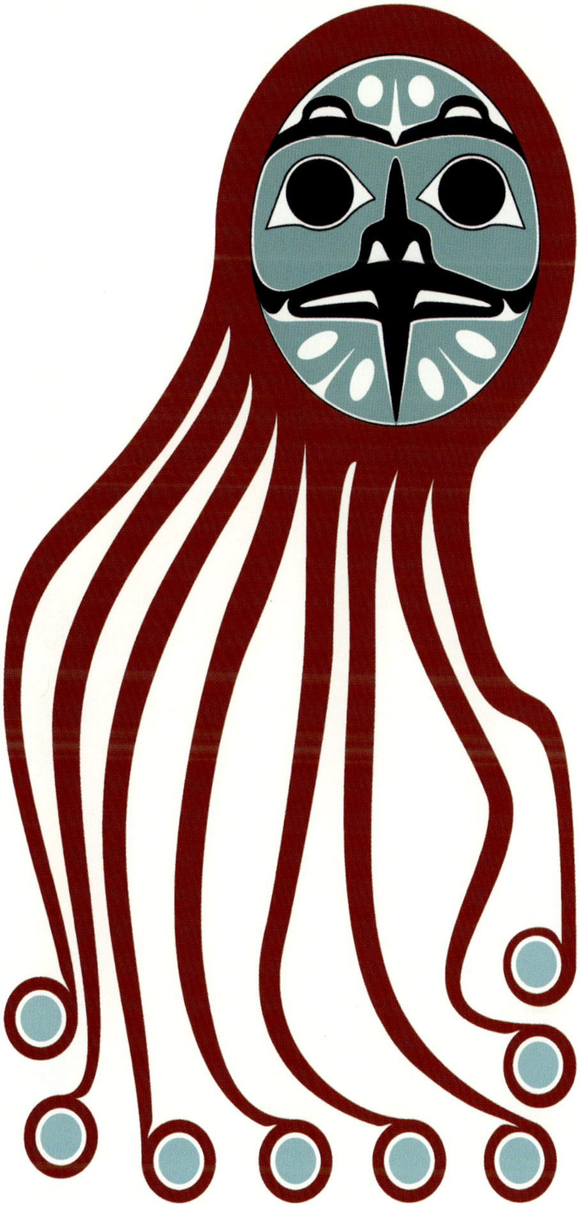

Inspired 2007 | *Octopus* 2007

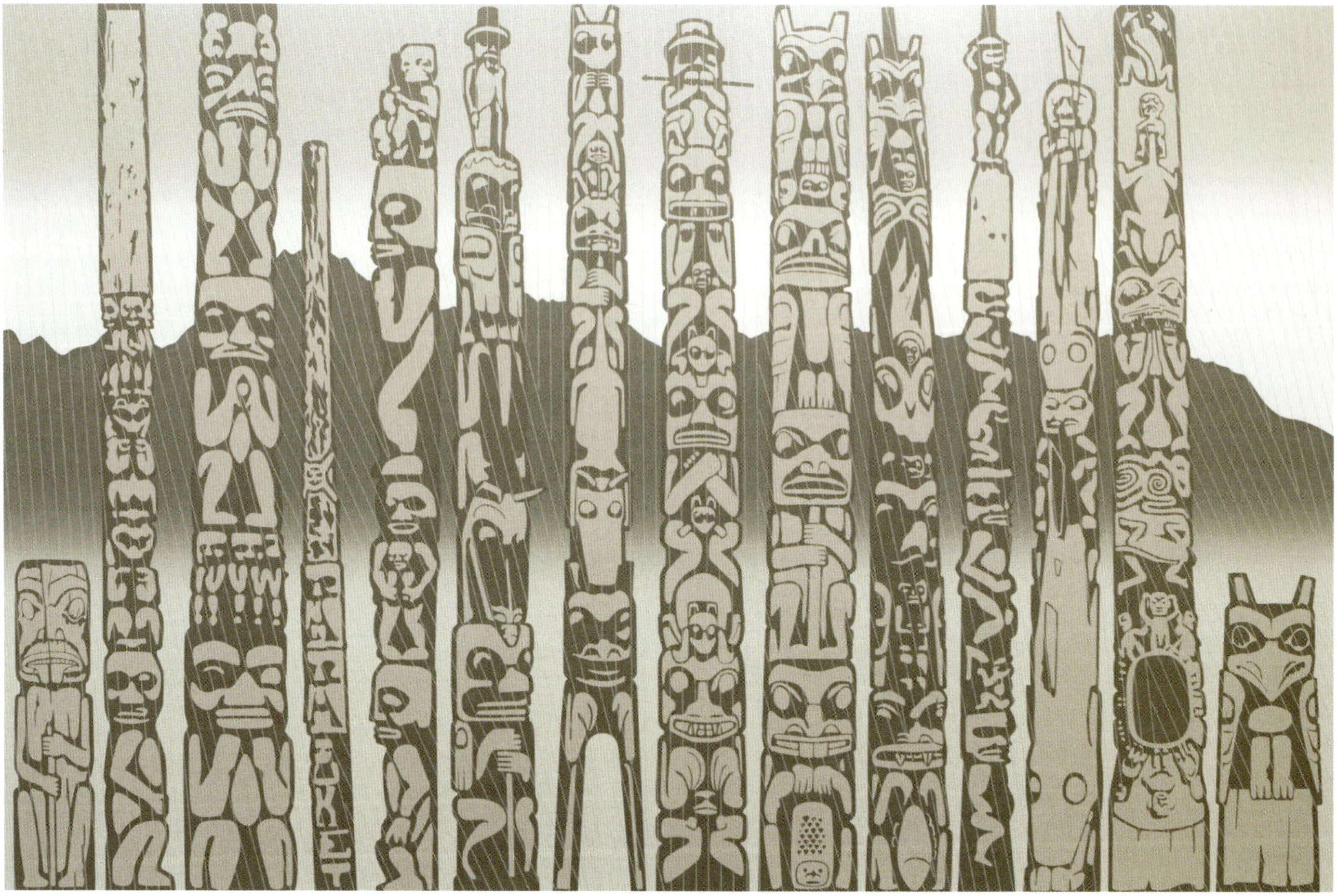

Back to the Land 2008

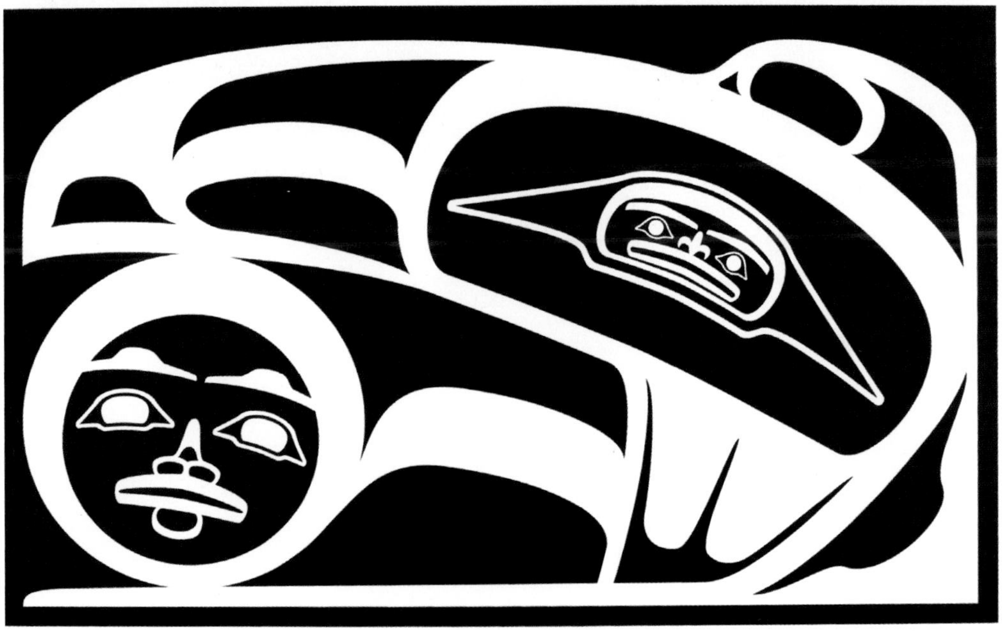

The Trickster 2010 | *The Creator* 2011

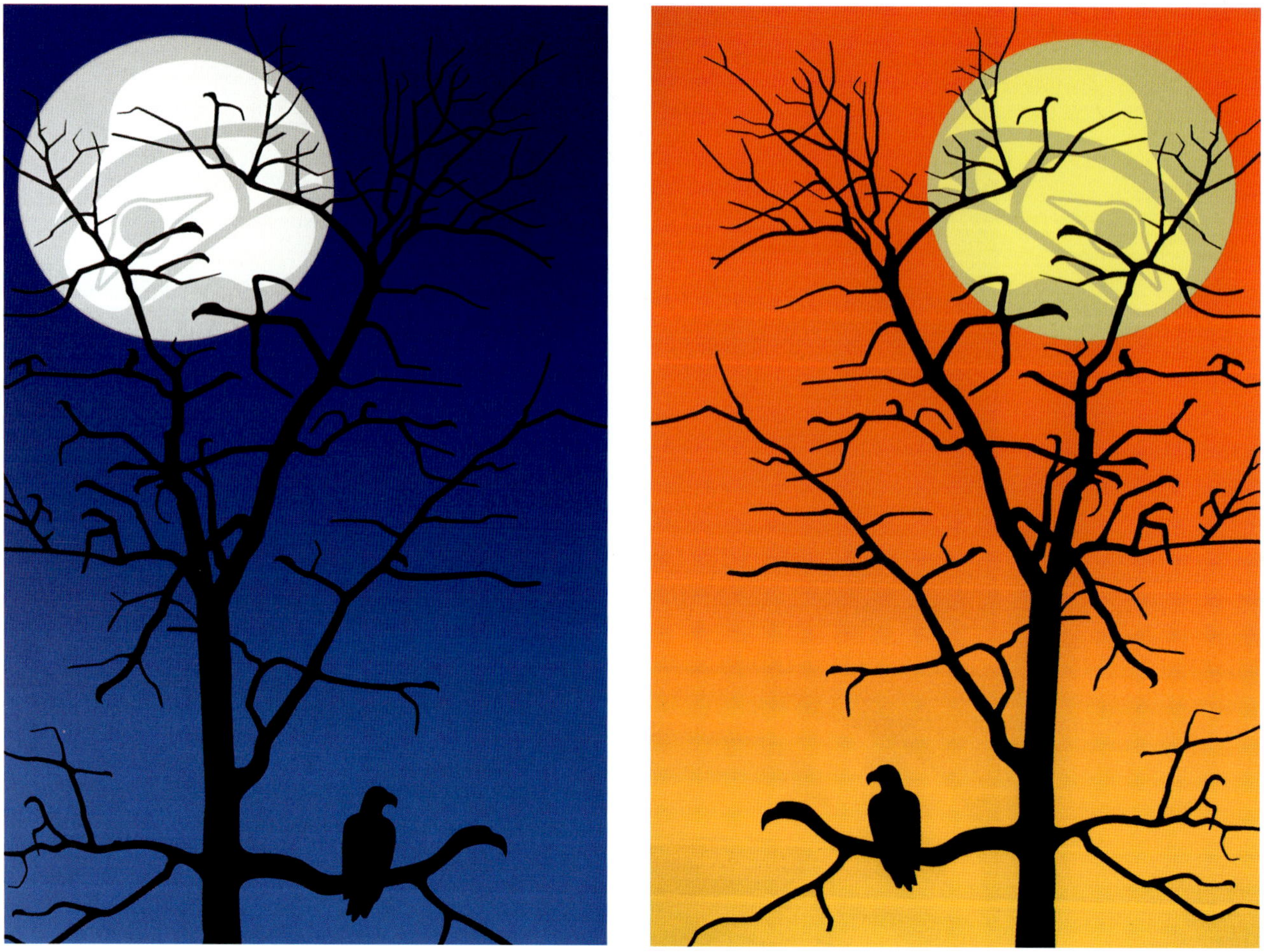

25 Eagles (Moonrise, Sunrise) 2011 | *Ktunaxa* 2011

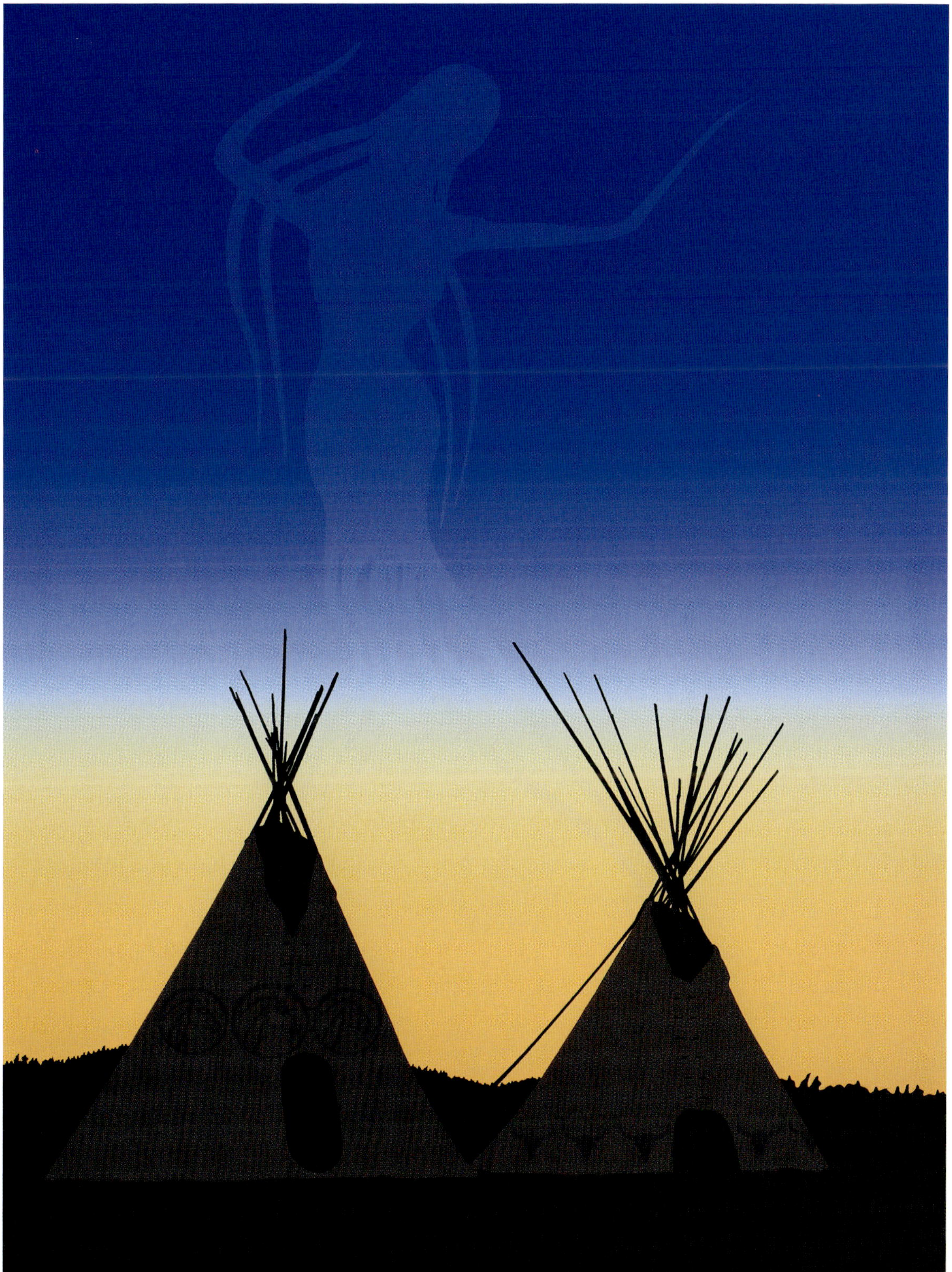

Huckleberry Eyes 2011

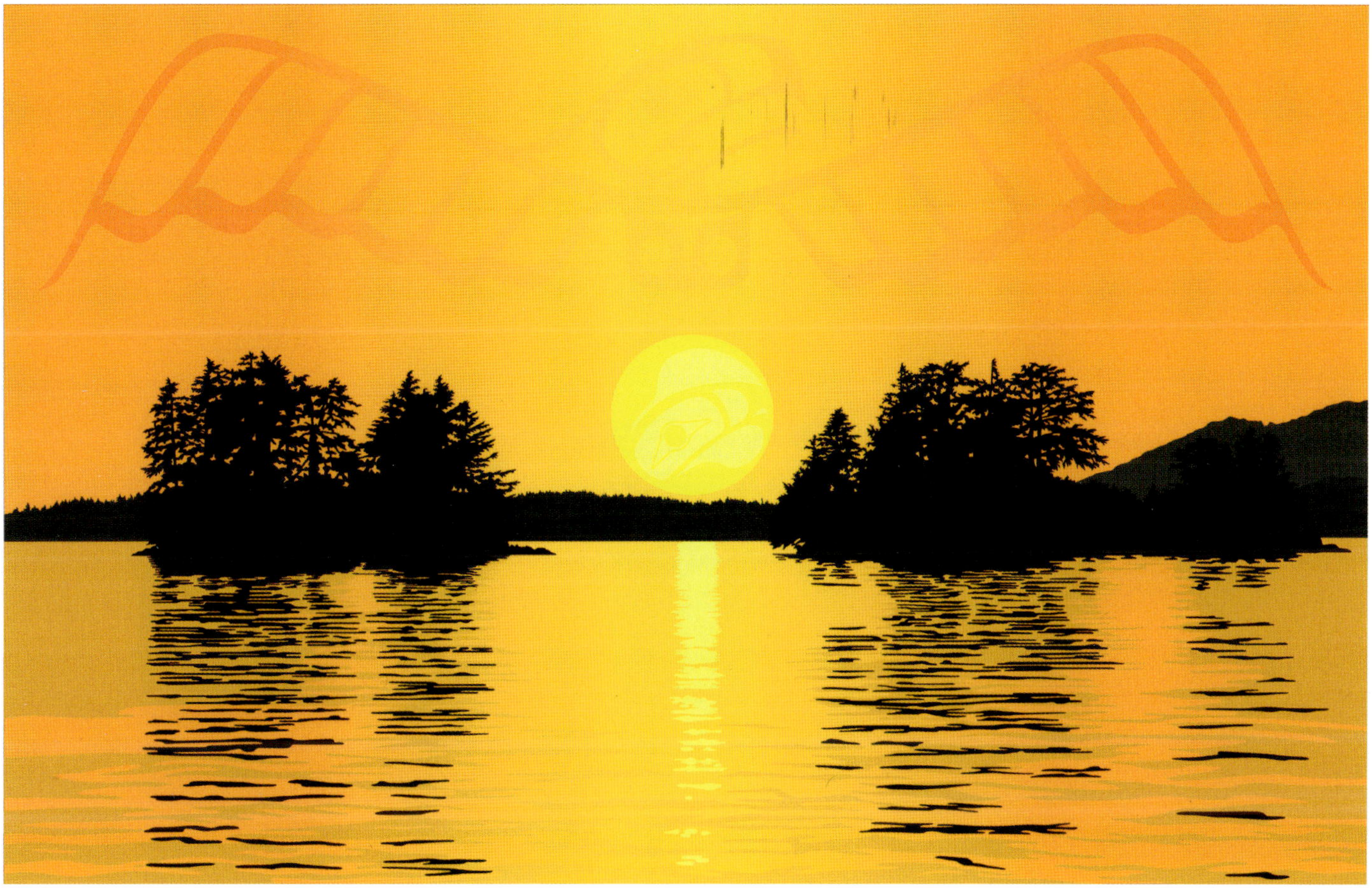

The Eagles of Deadman's Islets 2012

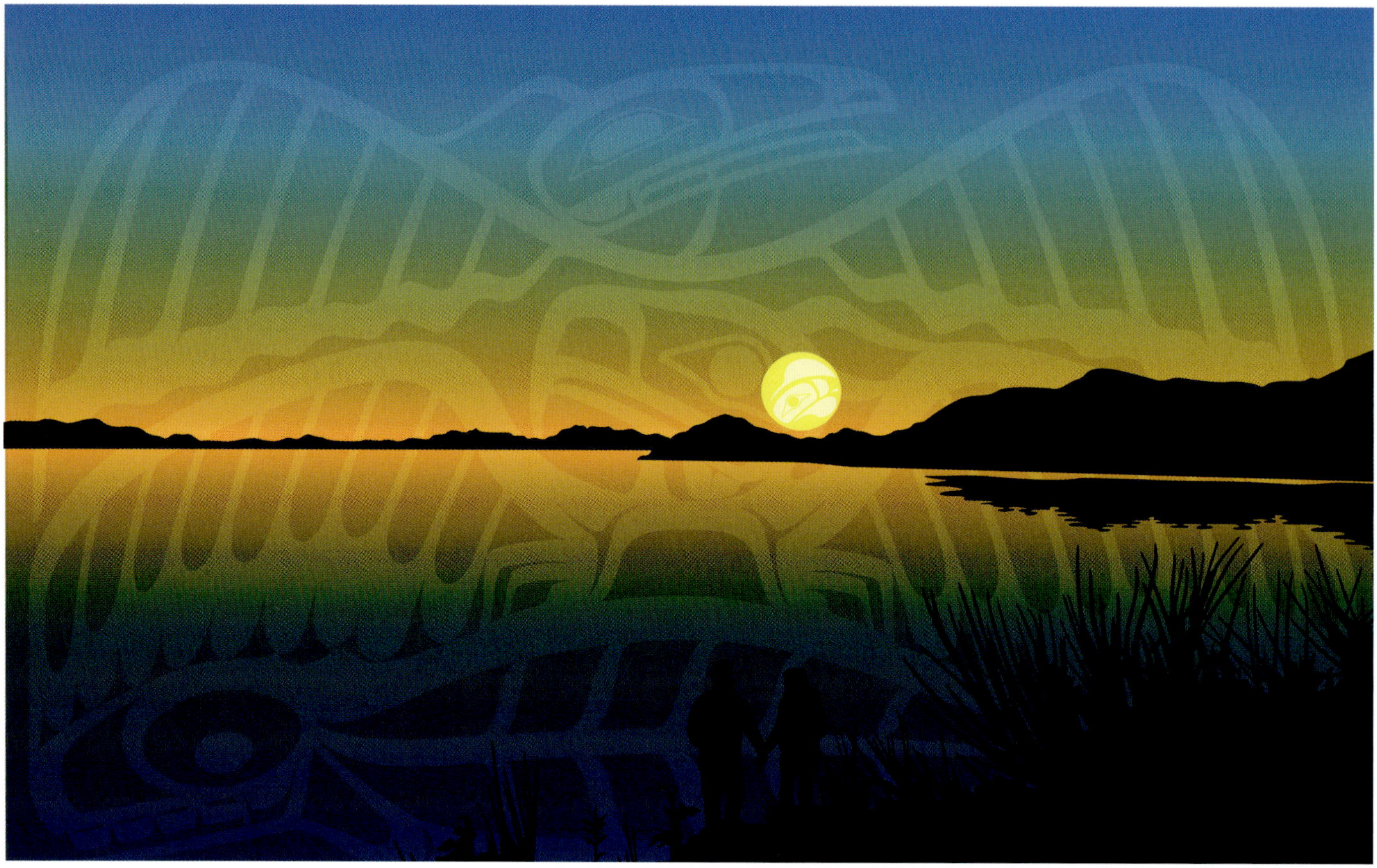

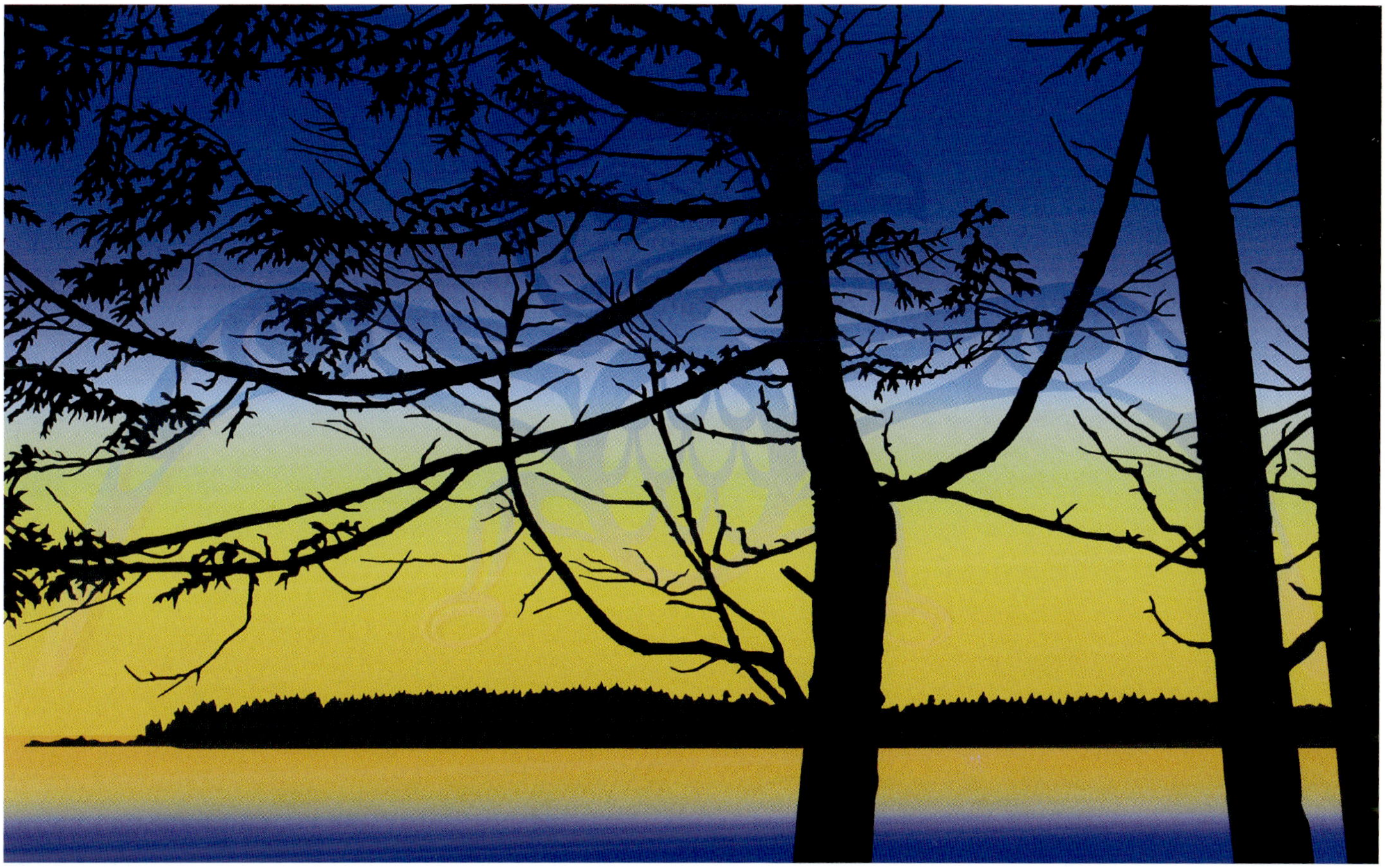

Echachis 2013

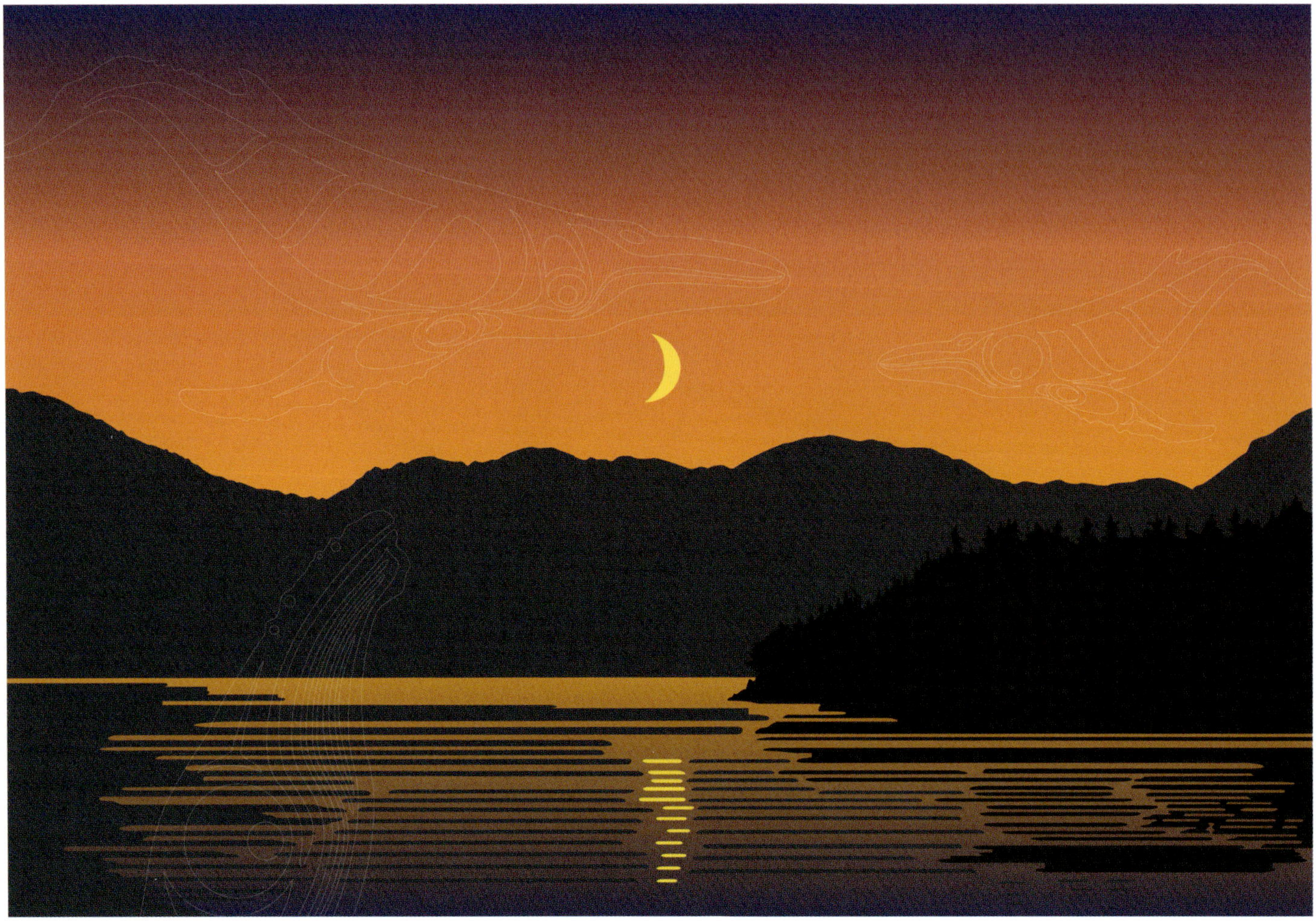

Whale Point 2013

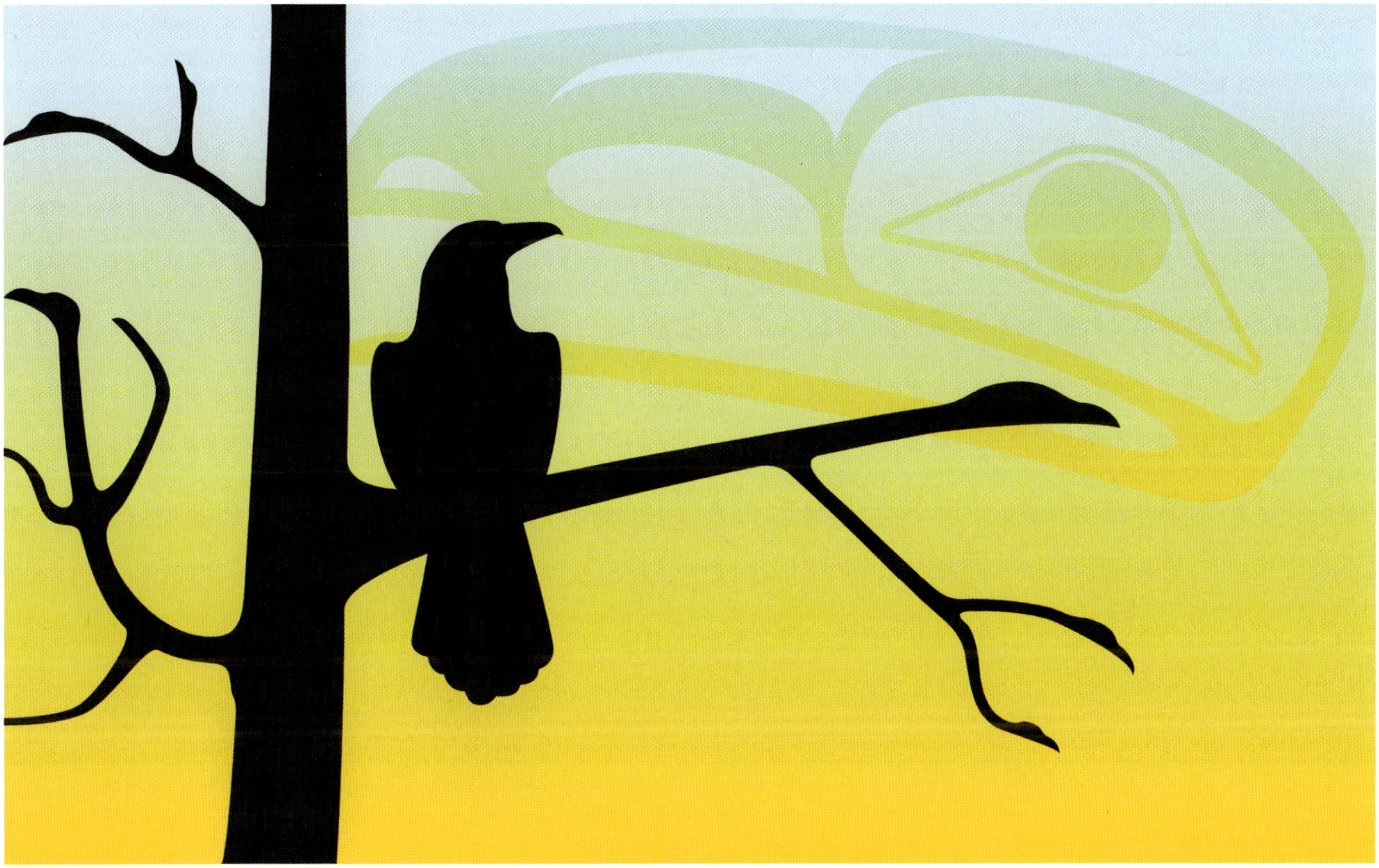

Raven in Tree 2013

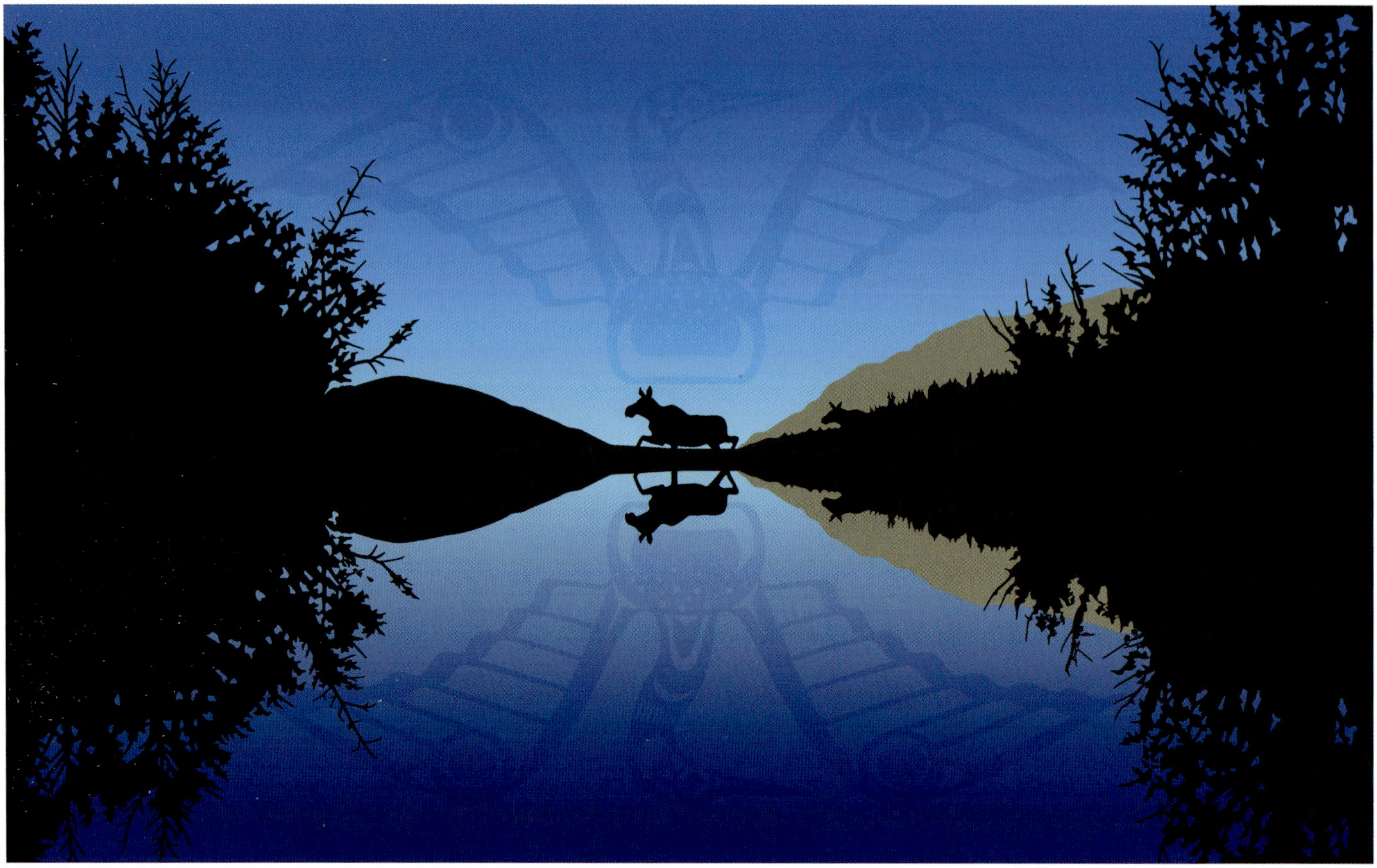

Mother Earth 2014

Wolf in the Fog 2014

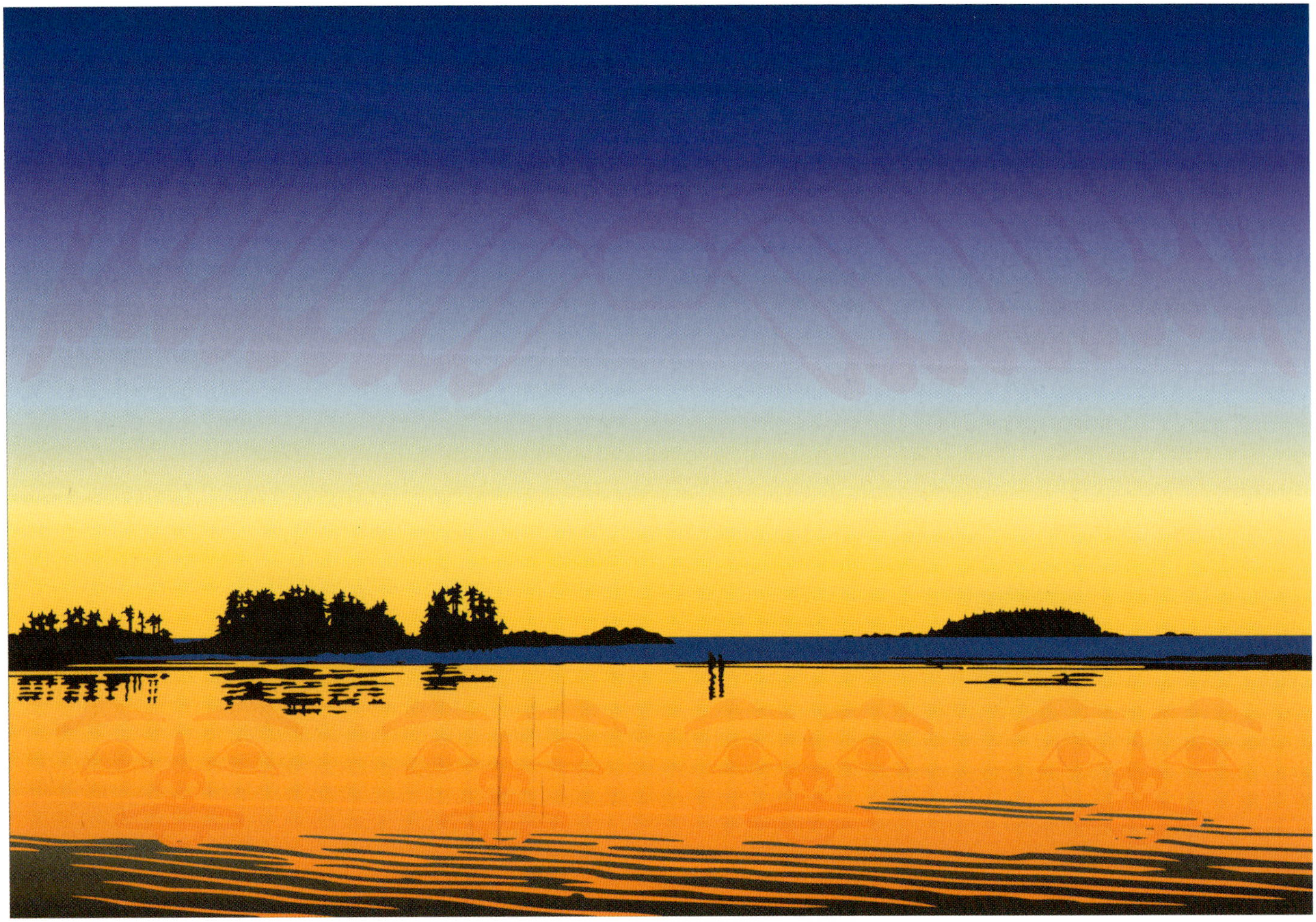

Last Light 2015

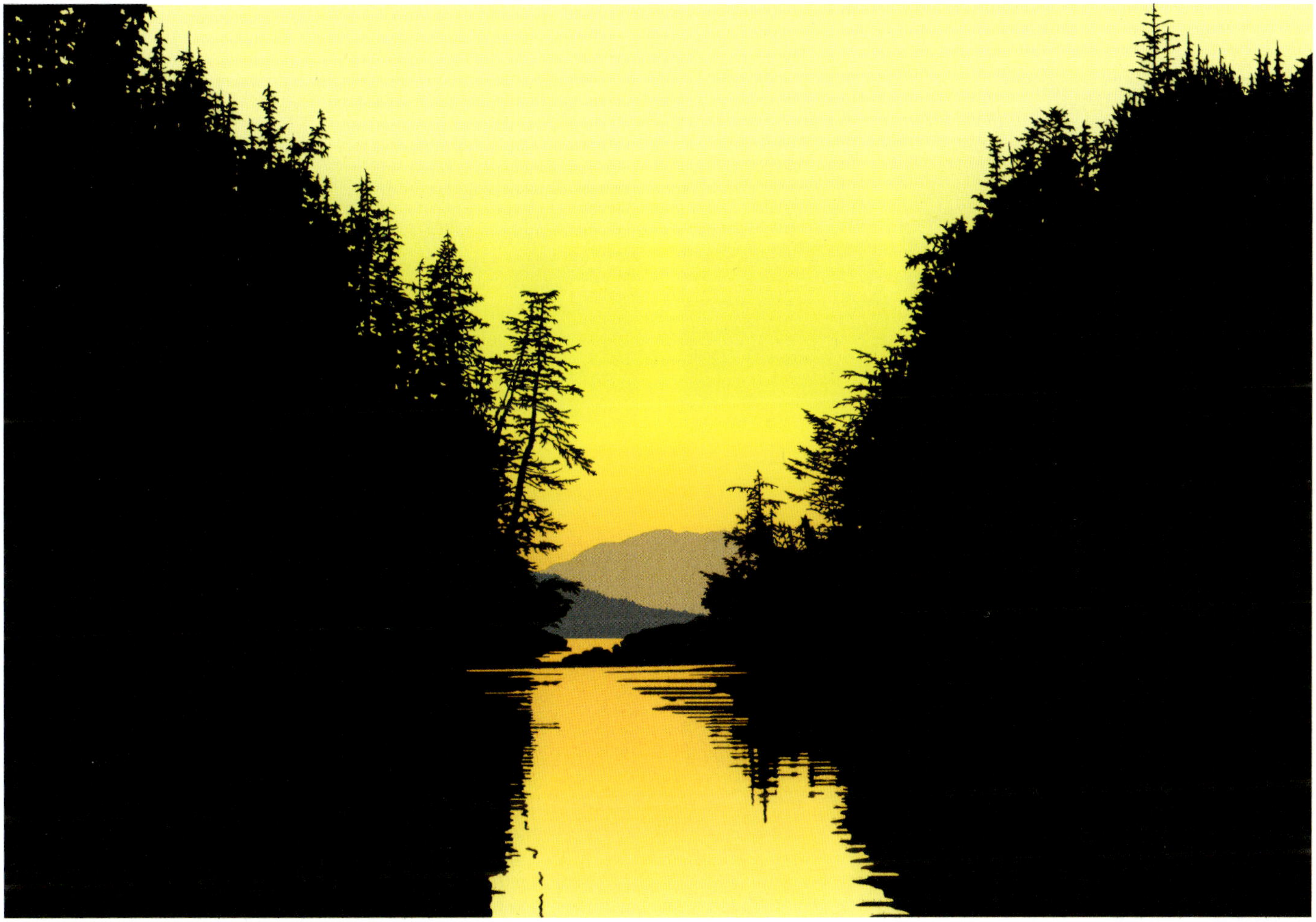

Great Bear Anchorage 2015

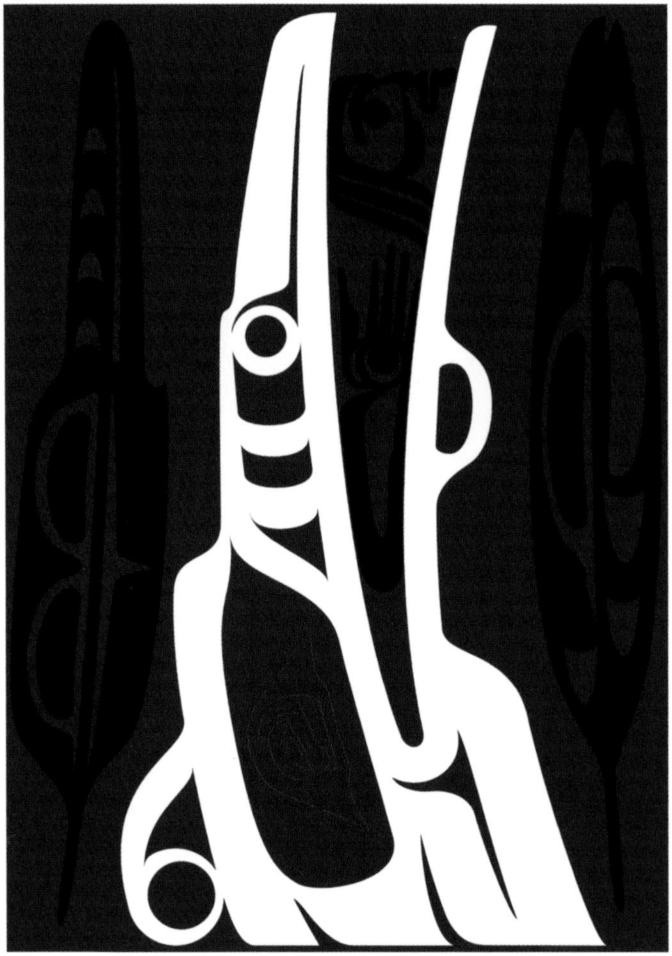

Big Raven 2017 | *Wolf and Cedar* 2017

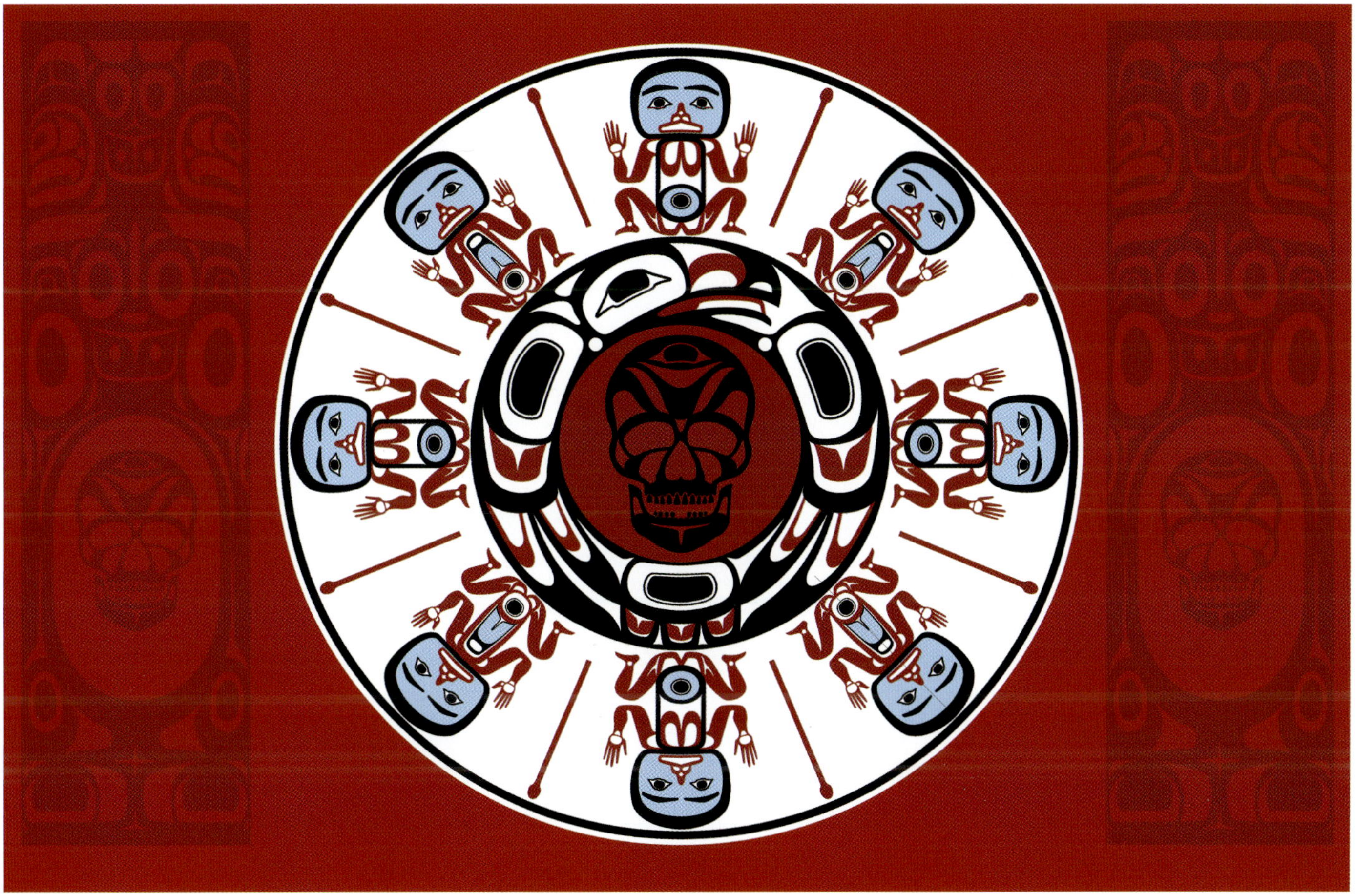

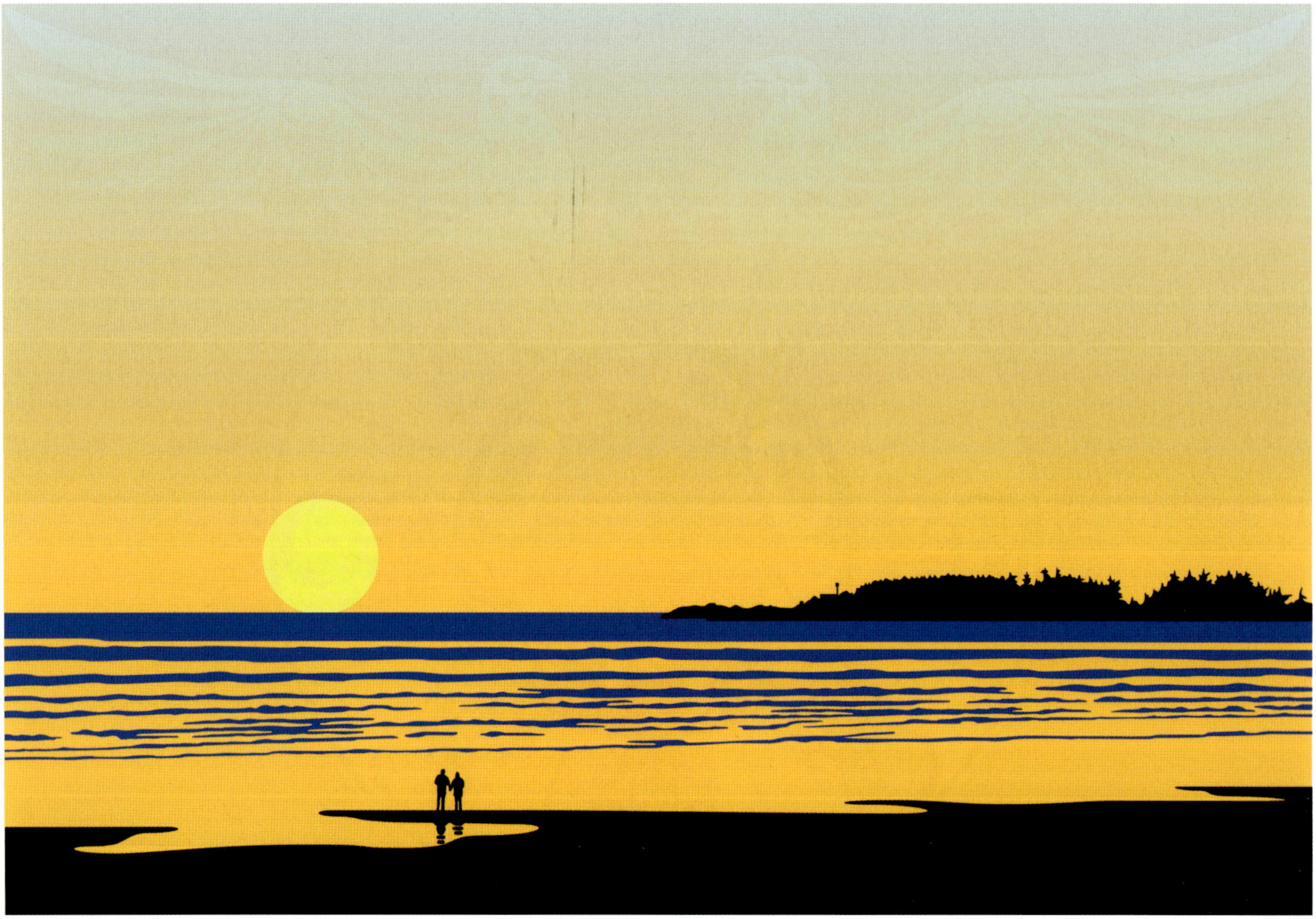

Courtship 2020

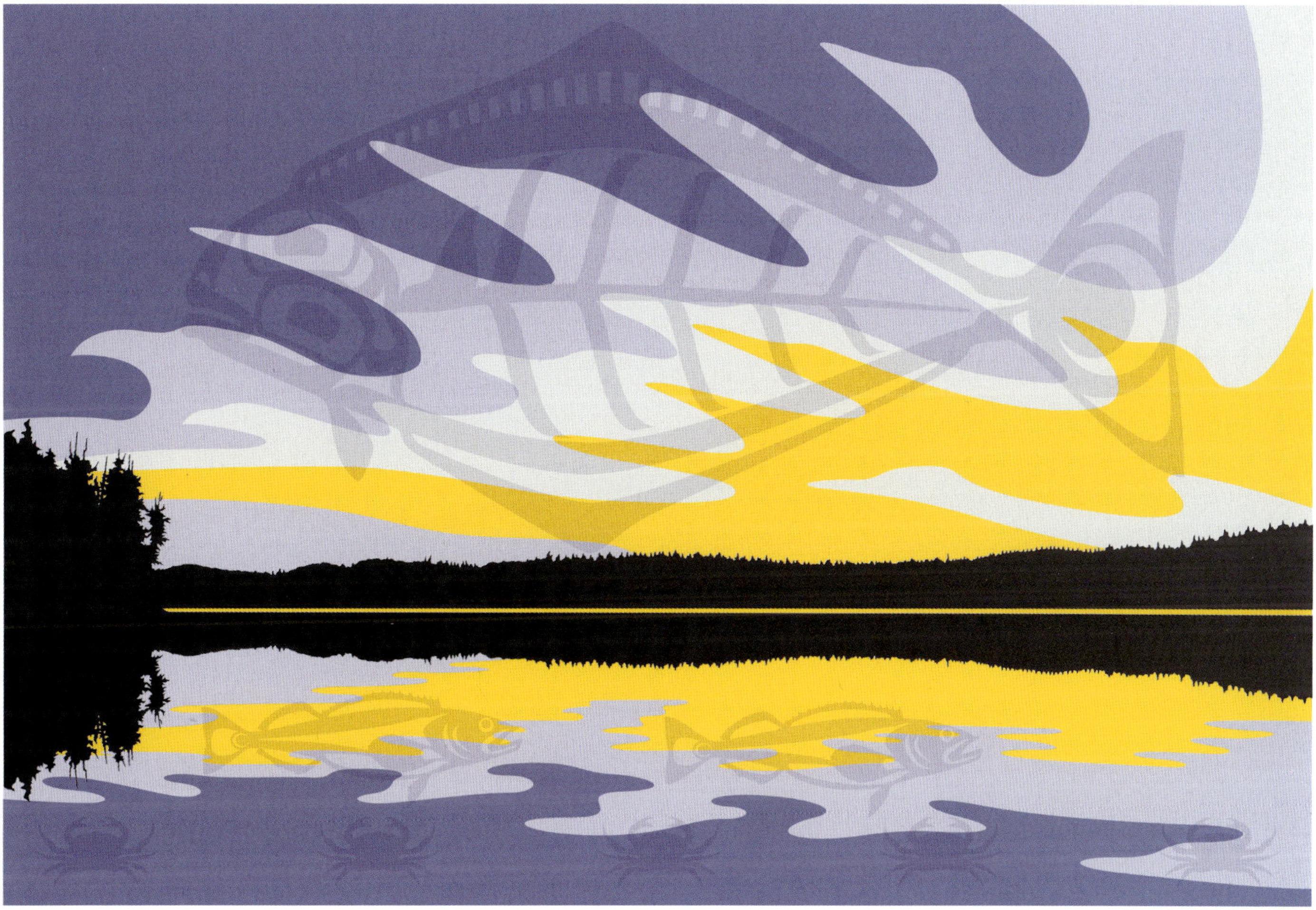

Billy Bay 2021

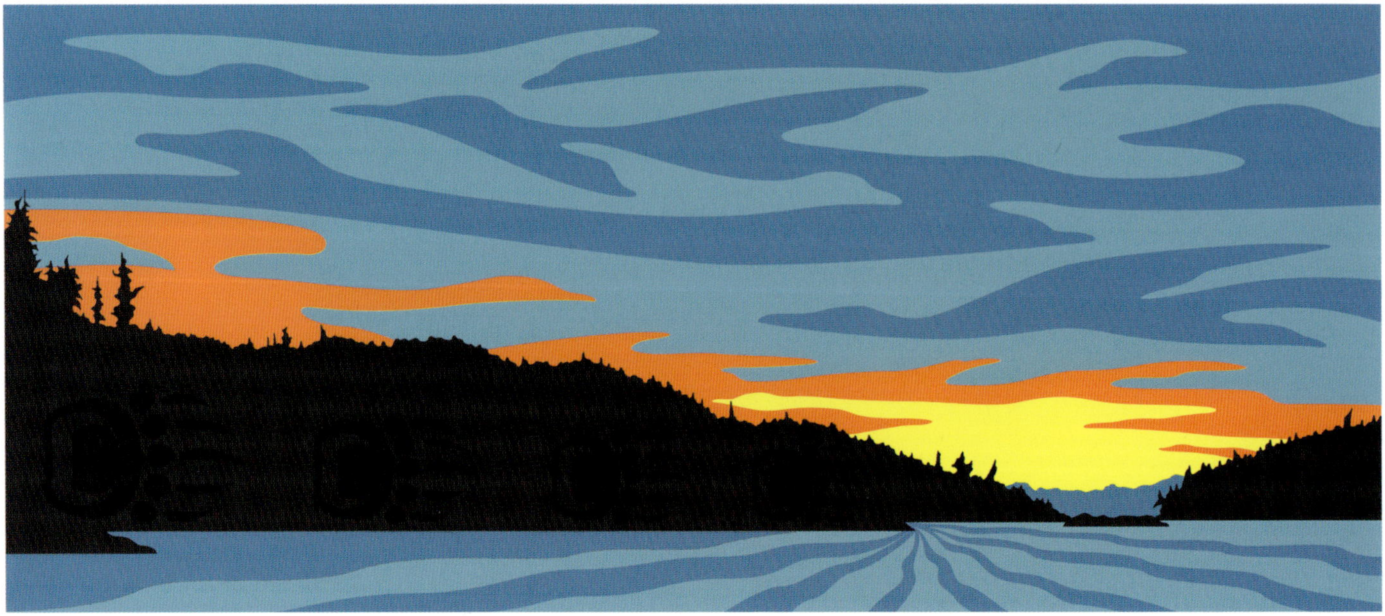

Last Anchorage 2022 | *Tidal Moon* 2024

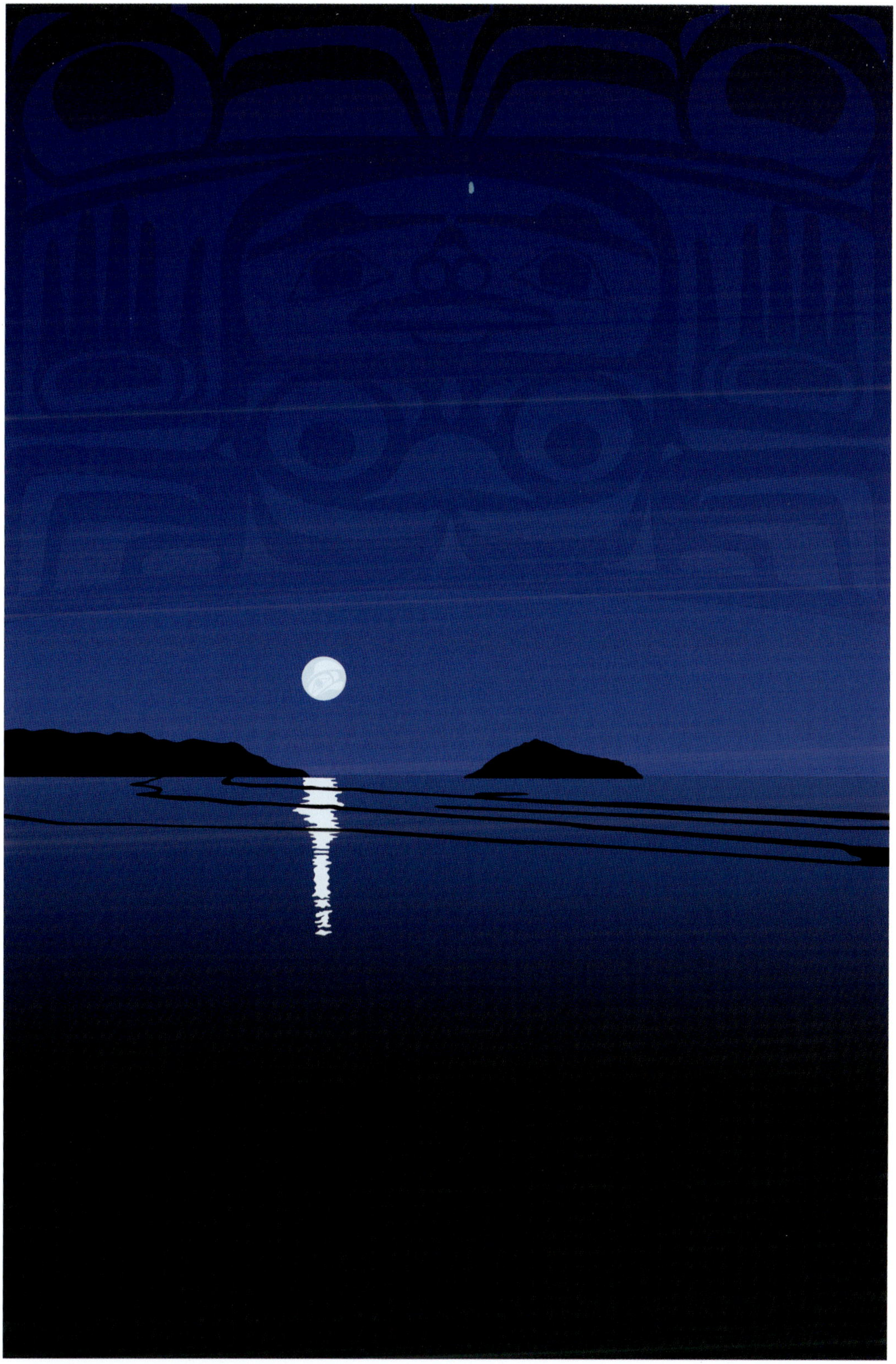

IMAGE CREDITS

Many of the photos of the art in this book were generously provided by a few sources.

The following images are part of the City of Burnaby Permanent Art Collection, gift of Natalie Freeman: *Tsimshian Woman* (p.5), *Tsimshian Chief* (p.5), *Raven with Clam* (p.17) and *Eagle with Chinook* (p.18). The use of these images is courtesy of the Burnaby Art Gallery.

The following images are part of the City of Burnaby Permanent Art Collection, gift of Lawrence Burr: *Stanley Park* (p.22), *Raven Dancer* (p.24), *Elegy* (p. 25), *Westcoast Sunset* (p.28), *Indian Summer* (p.29), *Spring Migration* (p.38), *Trial Island* (p.44), *Siwash Rock* (p.47), *Evening Anchorage* (p.48), *The Elders Are Watching* (p.49), *The Crossing* (p.52), *Kitkatla Winter* (p.54), *Kitkatla Spring* (p. 54), *The Homecoming* (p.55), *Megin Mist* (p.56), *Great Escape* (p.57), *Getting My Spirit Back* (p.60), *Totems at Dusk* (p.65), *King Pacific Sunset* (p.67) and *Milky Waters* (p.68). The use of these images is courtesy of the Burnaby Art Gallery.

Going To The Potlatch (p.36) is courtesy of the Inuit Gallery of Vancouver, photographed by Katsura Lee.

Photographs of *Oola! Oola!* (p.21), *The Westcoasters* (p.27), *Winter Fires* (p.32), *Steelhead* (p.34), *Cypre River* (p.37), *Sea Lions* (p.46) and *Midnight Rider* (p.61) are courtesy of Maynards Fine Art & Antiques, Richmond, BC.

All the rest are courtesy of the Eagle Aerie Gallery, the Roy Henry Vickers Archives, Daniela Petosa and Lucky Budd.

1 2 3 4 5 — 30 29 28 27 26

Harbour Publishing Co. Ltd.
P.O. Box 219, Madeira Park, BC, V0N 2H0
www.harbourpublishing.com

Project editor: Lucky Budd
Cover and text design by Jessica Sullivan, DSGN Dept.
Cover artwork: front, *Kitasoo Dawn*; back, *Skeena Crossing*
Printed and bound in South Korea

Canada

Canada Council for the Arts | Conseil des Arts du Canada | British Columbia Arts Council | British Columbia

Harbour Publishing acknowledges the support of the Canada Council for the Arts, the Government of Canada and the Province of British Columbia through the BC Arts Council.

Library and Archives Canada Cataloguing in Publication
Title: *The best of Roy Henry Vickers : 80 selected works /* foreword by Lucky Budd ; introduction by Roy Henry Vickers.
Names: Vickers, Roy Henry, 1946- author, artist | Budd, Lucky, 1976- writer of foreword
Identifiers: Canadiana 20260135941 | ISBN 9781998526635 (softcover)
Subjects: LCSH: Vickers, Roy Henry, 1946- | CSH: First Nations painting—British Columbia.
Classification: LCC ND249.V47 A4 2026 | DDC 759.11—dc23